THE CORPOREAL TURN

THE CORPOREAL TURN

PASSION, NECESSITY, POLITICS

JOHN TAMBORNINO

ROWMAN & LITTLEFIELD PUBLISHERS, INC.
Lanham • Boulder • New York • Oxford

ROWMAN & LITTLEFIELD PUBLISHERS, INC.

Published in the United States of America
by Rowman & Littlefield Publishers, Inc.
4720 Boston Way, Lanham, Maryland 20706
www.rowmanlittlefield.com

12 Hid's Copse Road
Cumnor Hill, Oxford OX2 9JJ, England

British Library Cataloguing in Publication Information Available

Library of Congress Cataloging-in-Publication Data

Tambornino, John, 1968–
    The corporeal turn : passion, necessity, politics / John Tambornino.
        p.   cm.
Includes bibliographical references and index.
    ISBN 0-7425-2156-7 (alk. paper) — ISBN 0-7425-2157-5 (pbk. : alk. paper)
    1. Body, Human—Social aspects.   2. Body, Human—Political aspects.
I. Title.
    HM636 .T36   2002
    306.4—dc21

                                                                    2002001801

Printed in the United States of America

♾ ™
        The paper used in this publication meets the minimum requirements of
American National Standard for Information Sciences—Permanence of Paper for
Printed Library Materials, ANSI/NISO Z39.48–1992.

CONTENTS

ACKNOWLEDGMENTS

Had my high school English teacher Lane Page not introduced me to the life of thinking, I might not be writing these acknowledgments. While I was an undergraduate at Macalester College, Henry West further introduced me to this life, and to moral and political philosophy in particular. Karen Warren challenged me to deepen my thinking and to elevate my writing. Sanford Schram impressed upon me the subtleties and complexities of politics and political thinking. Steve Cohen, though deciding not to pursue an academic path, has from the day we met been a source of stimulation and a voice of clarity. While I was a graduate student, a variety of institutional support from the University of Minnesota and Johns Hopkins University provided the material conditions that thinking requires.

Since devoting myself to political theory, I have benefited from the company, attention, and encouragement of far too many individuals to identify in this space. Portions of this volume have benefited from the critical commentary of Talal Asad, Jane Bennett, Richard Bett, Lisa Disch, Russell Fox, Jason Frank, Ivan Grabovac, Bonnie Honig, Rebecca Plant, Stephen Schneck, Giulia Sissa, Tracy Strong, Linda Zerilli, and the editors of the *Journal of Political Philosophy*. Portions have also been presented at the 1996 Northeastern Political Science Association Annual Meeting, the Annual Graduate Student Conference at the Institute of the Liberal Arts, Emory University, the 1997 Annual Meeting of the American Political Science Association, and the 1998 Annual Meeting for the Northeastern Political Science Association. I thank the organizers for these opportunities and the audiences for their interest. I have also benefited from the comments and advice of Tarak Barkawi, Frank Browning, Matthew Crenson, Mary Dietz, Samantha Frost, Benjamin Ginsberg, Ed Ingebretsen, Morris Kaplan, Jerome Schneewind, Morton Schoolman, and Scott Sherer. Stuart Hampshire kindly read an earlier version of the chapter that discusses his writings. Staff at Rowman & Littlefield were splendid, as they guided, prodded, and corrected me at crucial points. I am especially thankful to my editors, Stephen Wrinn and Mary Carpenter, and to my copyeditor, Cheryl Hoffman, for their interest and efforts.

My greatest debts are to Richard Flathman and William Connolly. From the moment we met, Richard Flathman has addressed me as a colleague. He has been generous with his time and suggestions and constantly encouraging, and he often has illuminated the dark corners into which my thinking not infrequently leads me. William Connolly has been equally encouraging. He and I have had the pleasure of exploring many of these ideas simultaneously, in a manner that, I hope, has been to his benefit also. But most often I have been trailing his rapid lead, absorbing his enthusiasm, and wandering onto paths he chose not to take.

Finally, a few individuals distant from political theory deserve thanks. Rebecca Plant, in her nonacademic capacities, provided warmth and good company. Chris Elcock tolerated me when I was writing and, even more amazingly, when I was having trouble writing. Jeffrey Jacobson has been a consistent source of chaos and laughter. And of the support from my family, my grandparents John and Carmen Sheriden have been especially generous and patient. I dedicate this book to them.

INTRODUCTION

THE CORPOREAL TURN

When we ignore the body, we are more easily victimized by it.
—Milan Kundera

When investigating the experiences of dislocation, loss, and brutality by many Chinese during the Cultural Revolution, medical anthropologists Arthur Kleinman and Joan Kleinman found bodily experience to be inseparable from political authority, cultural values, and social change.[1] Most curiously, during periods in which there were few outlets for political criticism, "criticism" seemed to be manifest as "neurasthenia—a common syndrome of chronic pain, sleeplessness, fatigue, dizziness, and related physical symptoms, as well as sadness, anxiety, and anger" (714). Patients attributed this to the revolution, speaking at once of specific bodily ailments; of unforgettable memories of public reprimand, forced self-criticism, and beatings; and of generalized fear, alienation, and disorientation. "Each complaint, elaborated in the context of a story that integrated social and bodily suffering, was a moral commentary . . . [on] the delegitimation of Chinese society" (716). Discussing their suffering often led patients to more articulate political criticism, which in turn helped to alleviate their pain and modify their bodily experience.

Kleinman and Kleinman maintain that even their broad, interdisciplinary approach, which incorporates medicine, anthropology, history, and social theory, is insufficient for comprehending such phenomena. Such

1

phenomena also elude much of recent political theory, as do important aspects of being, scientific and cultural developments, and dimensions of politics involving the body. Indeed, in comparison to the concern for the body pervading past philosophy and political thought, in contemporary political theory the concern is muted.

Recent political science, especially with the growing prominence of rational choice theory, also pays little heed to the body and related concerns, although earlier works such as Gabriel Almond and Sidney Verba's *Civic Culture* did display such an interest. Rather than limiting their analysis to cognition, belief, and ideology, Almond and Verba viewed modulating the "flow of feelings," "managing affect," and discouraging "emotional withdrawal" from legitimate institutions as crucial elements in governance and citizenship.[2] Their insights are valuable, and it is unfortunate that they have been forgotten. Nevertheless, there are limits to discussions such as Almond and Verba's, as they join behaviorists in failing to appreciate fully the layers and complexity of affect, the extent to which it is linguistically and conceptually constituted, and the varying means by which it is managed and can be modified.

A number of political theorists and philosophers have recently called for greater attention to the body. Stanley Cavell, Jean Cohen, William Connolly, Jean Elshtain, Martha Nussbaum, Hilary Putnam, Bernard Williams, and Iris Marion Young have emphasized the need to rethink conceptions of subjectivity, reflection, and ethics in light of bodily experience, cultural developments, and scientific findings. Yet few of these calls have been followed by sustained attention.[3]

In the past few years the body has received considerable attention from such fields as American studies, anthropology, feminist theory, history, law, literature, philosophy, and sociology.[4] Yet much of this literature fails to fully appreciate embodiment. In particular, much of the discussion of the body, especially in gender and cultural studies, focuses almost exclusively on *representations* of the body. This focus, conceptually and substantively, tends to emphasize language, belief, and symbolic systems while overlooking affect, disposition, and disciplinary practices; to emphasize representations or constructions of the self without exploring *tactics* of the self. As a result, such discussions of the body neglect crucial aspects of embodiment—

aspects that, by their very nature, do not lend themselves to representation.[5]

The writings of Judith Butler, perhaps the most influential theorist discussing the body today, illustrate how the body can be obscured by focus on representation. When asked recently to comment on this possibility and to explore the corporeal dimensions of discourse, performativity, and subjectivity, Butler expressed reluctance. She concedes that it is a mistake to lapse into a "complete linguisticism," in which language is all, but then maintains that attending to that which exceeds language risks viewing language as simply representing independent objects.[6] Yet Butler's opposition is overdrawn, as I shall make evident by combining criticism of representational conceptions of language *with* attention to aspects of embodiment exceeding language.

When exploring corporeality and politics, the challenge is to focus on those practices and types of experience that do not lend themselves to explicit, conscious attention. It is to foreground the body without relegating language, culture, and consciousness to the background. Indeed, the greatest challenge is to explore the intersections between the body, language, culture, and consciousness. Meeting this challenge would amount to a *corporeal* turn.

A corporeal turn involves focusing on complex relations, layered combinations, and indiscernible zones between corporeality and culture, embodiment and discipline, techniques and governance, and affect and sensibility. The complexity and relative indiscernibility of these relationships present both challenges and opportunities. Challenges, because explication of these relationships is likely to feel insufficient, and because it modifies them, thus requiring new explication. Opportunities, because appreciating the complexity of these relationships may enable us to act upon them more effectively, and because zones of indiscernibility may contribute to creativity and innovation in politics.

In order to make a corporeal turn, I examine Hannah Arendt, Charles Taylor, Friedrich Nietzsche, and Stuart Hampshire. Nietzsche, though often praised by Richard Rorty and others for his linguistic turn, more fundamentally made a corporeal turn. His considerations of language are part of his larger attempt to move beyond what he saw as centuries of neglect and disparagement of the body, contending that philosophy heretofore has been "merely an interpretation of the body and a *misunderstanding of the body.*"[7]

I begin, however, not with Nietzsche but with two thinkers greatly influenced by him, Arendt and Taylor. Both give sustained attention to corporeality and illuminate numerous issues, but their aversion to certain aspects of corporeality is bound up with their aversion to certain themes in Nietzsche. Thus, attention to the themes in Nietzsche that they neglect helps to expose aspects of corporeality that they neglect. My discussion of Nietzsche also prepares the way for my subsequent discussion of Hampshire, who shares much of Nietzsche's views on corporeality while diverging significantly in matters of ethics and politics. I proceed, then, not chronologically but thematically, as my interest is not in the historical development of these issues. Rather, I work through diverse, increasingly promising treatments of corporeality and politics in order to fashion a perspective of my own. The sequence I have chosen, given my questions and concerns, allows greater thematic continuity than would a chronological sequence.

Unlike many of the contemporary thinkers who do attend to corporeality, the thinkers I have chosen relate their treatments to traditional political concerns such as community, authority, freedom, and conflict. Another reason for concentrating on these thinkers, rather than on those the reader might expect, such as Gilles Deleuze and Luce Irigaray, is that they are familiar thinkers whose attention to corporeality remains less familiar. The fact that corporeality has received little attention in thinkers who are extensively discussed itself supports my contention that corporeality is easily overlooked. I give little space to thinkers who most neglect or disparage the body. My strongest criticisms—those directed at Arendt—may extend to thinkers such as Plato and Kant, whom Arendt herself criticizes for their negative orientations to the body. Similarly, many of my criticisms of Arendt pertain to influential contemporary thinkers, such as John Rawls and Jürgen Habermas, whose positions (especially such notions as the "original position" and the "ideal speech situation") are more Kantian than Arendt's.

Michel Foucault has greatly influenced my thinking on these matters, yet I do not discuss him at length. At the point where a reader might anticipate discussion of Foucault (after Nietzsche), I turn to Hampshire. As a postwar analytic philosopher, Hampshire effectively probed the limits of his discipline and pressed others to consider neglected Continental philosophers, particularly Spinoza. By the 1970s many of those who had been inspired by Hampshire turned their attention to emerging Continental thinkers, and his influence waned. Yet he should not be forgotten. He anticipated recent materialist formulations in philosophy of mind and linked these formulations to questions of ethics and politics to an extent no other thinker has. His portrait of "techniques of the body" complements Foucault's "care of the self" and clarifies issues that Foucault identified as critical but did not live to treat fully, such as the relation of symbolic systems to material practices in subjectivity and ethics. These reflections lead Hampshire to an unusually subtle liberalism—which neither conventional liberals nor critics of liberalism have fully engaged—discrediting the claim that liberalism necessarily presumes a disembodied, rational subject. His writings are a rich resource that is barely tapped, so I devote an entire chapter to begin to do this.

Arendt, Taylor, Nietzsche, and Hampshire each pursue a tremendous range of philosophical and political issues. Their treatments of the body are not confined neatly in their thinking but rather are pervasive. Instead of isolating a single, readily accessible problem or question, they grapple with entangled themes and clusters of concerns. The following pairs, though varying in terminology and formulation, reside in these thinkers and condense many of my concerns. I list them to convey how fundamental and far-reaching treatment of the body must be, to open my considerations rather than to foreclose them.

Necessity and Freedom. Bound up with many discussions of the body is the distinction between necessity and freedom, with the body typically relegated to the domain of necessity. This is most pronounced in Arendt, for whom the body, with its constant demands and inherent limits, epitomizes necessity. In order to secure freedom, Arendt eventually joins the long line of thinkers who appeal to the will. Willfulness is seen as the capacity for action that is not mere reaction, for initiation that is not reducible to material causation, for innovation that eludes explanation. Yet when the will is introduced in order to secure freedom, both are placed in tension with, and often in opposition to, the body. The domain of freedom—of

"natality" and "becoming," of the unanticipated and the unprecedented—
is then contrasted with the domain of bodily necessity. Once matters are
formulated in this manner, attending to freedom requires little attention
to the body.

Taylor, rather than opposing freedom to bodily necessity, conceives freedom as "attunement" between our highest aspirations and our basic needs.
He alleviates the tension between the will and the body by assuming a
"direction in being" inherent in the world and in human embodiment. For
Nietzsche, the will is neither independent of the body nor contrasted with
bodily necessity. Rather, willfulness is produced by *intensive organization*
of the body, enabling agency, volition, and individuality. Instead of opposing freedom to bodily necessity, Hampshire coils them closely. For him,
freedom often involves identifying that regarded as necessity and attempting to modify it by tactical means. Explanation of necessity itself can
become an act of freedom, enhancing and reconfiguring it. Such a position
is especially promising today, as our abilities to modify bodily necessity
and to explain bodily activity rapidly advance.

Need and Desire. Close to the distinction between necessity and freedom is
that between need and desire. Need—precisely that which is necessary, and
for this reason is compelling and not freely chosen—is often grounded in
the matrix of basic bodily needs. Needs are often seen as essential and stable, as opposed to desires, which are more contingent and variable. Arendt
views the identification and satisfaction of needs as relatively simple. This is
much less the case for Taylor, and less so still for Hampshire. And for Nietzsche, identifying stable needs, even the most basic, is deeply problematical.

All four thinkers, however, see desire as more problematical than need.
Desire refers not only to that which we *want* but also to that which we want
so strongly as to seem to *need*. As Taylor elaborates, desires are more complex than basic bodily needs, as they are less easily identified and articulated and often remain inchoate and ambiguous. Taylor responds to this difficulty by introducing a loose hierarchy of values to order needs and desires.
Yet contrary to Taylor's ideal, as Hampshire emphasizes, desires, once identified and articulated, often are not easily satisfied, as they may conflict with
basic needs.

Hampshire joins Nietzsche in emphasizing that attempts to satisfy particular needs and desires, given their conflictual and controversial nature, involves exclusive, dubious choices between them. Since desires, especially across individuals, vary and conflict more than do needs, greater efforts are required to consolidate and contain them. As Foucault illustrates, such efforts often require extensive, ongoing discipline and normalization. Taylor's ideal of community must come to terms with the pervasiveness of discipline and normalization. Arendt's ideal of politics and Nietzsche's ideal of individuality must come to terms with their indispensability. And Hampshire's ideal of effective interventions must come to terms with the corporeal limits to discipline and normalization.

Nature and Convention. In distinguishing necessity from freedom, and what we truly need from what we merely desire, Arendt, Taylor, and Hampshire variously distinguish nature from convention. Nature is seen as prior to, or independent of, things we make, as providing constraints we do not choose, whereas convention consists of that which we make and choose. This distinction is strongest in Arendt, for whom nature is the domain of necessity and convention ("the common world") is that of freedom. For Taylor, nature is a source of value and meaning that provides ethical orientation and sustenance.

Yet, as Hampshire emphasizes, it is *human* nature, stemming from our capacity for thought, to introduce artifice into nature. It is our nature to establish conventions, to impose constraints that are always to some extent counter to our nature. Morality—a set of conventions and constraints—is in this sense *un*natural; it contains and does violence to nature as it enables and protects humanity. Morality allows development and flourishing while stifling them. It prevents injury and suffering while giving rise to them. The challenge is to establish a morality that is felt to be less injurious and that causes less suffering, that meets our needs while allowing us to satisfy our desires, that consists of constraints that are also enabling. This challenge leads Taylor to search for a "design" or "bent" in nature, to be expressed in morality and conventions. Morality and conventions that stem from nature are viewed as not *merely* conventional but as "authentic." In pursuing them, Taylor is often not alert to signs that nature does not conform to his bent.

Nietzsche strays furthest from the distinction between nature and convention, without dispensing with it entirely. He assumes nature to be neither directed by telos nor wholly governed by law. Rather, nature is like convention, in that its "gaps" make it forever unstable, unfinished, and subject to alteration. Even "instincts"—those aspects of the self felt to be most natural—are an uncertain mixture of nature and convention.

Mortality and Transcendence. To be corporeal is to be mortal. Arendt emphasizes that upon realizing our mortality we search for something that transcends it. In her reading, Western religion and philosophy have been principally concerned with transcendence, with giving meaning to human life, suffering, and mortality by appealing to that which is above or beyond them. For Arendt, individual mortality is best transcended by political action—words and deeds that promise not eternity but immortality. In the modern era, in which life is the highest value and pleasure the chief pursuit, such action is said to have become rare. Yet in valorizing political action Arendt neglects the concerns of ordinary life. Taylor appreciates ordinary life, while contending that it requires sources of meaning that transcend life. A life without such sources is said to be shallow.

For Nietzsche, transcendence occurs, to the extent that it does, not through political action or spiritual meaning but through "self-overcoming," when individuals transcend their earlier limits and set new ones. Central to ethics is an orientation to the one limit that cannot be transcended—mortality—an orientation that does not view it as at odds with a meaningful life but incorporates acceptance of death into affirmation of life. Indeed, mortality *allows* for a meaningful life, as it is only within this limit (in which there is not time for everything, so a few things can be done and the rest must be forgone) that choice and affirmation have significance. Hampshire avoids any notion of the transcendental, believing that it leads to an obfuscating "extra-materialism" and to ethical commitments that place something higher than individual concerns and the preservation of human life. Yet eventually he concludes that an ethic of life provides insufficient bases for the preservation of life, and he is led to search for ethical standards that transcend any individual.

Reason and Passion. Discussions of the body often are bound up with a distinction between reason and passion, as is the case with these thinkers. Whereas reason suggests uniformity, rule, and consensus, passion suggests variability, unruliness, and conflict. Taylor distinguishes reason and passion less sharply and strives for their alignment; he is led to this by assuming passions to be, or able to become, less variable, unruly, and conflictual. Yet Taylor joins the other thinkers in viewing passions as compelling, as involving forces seemingly outside ourselves and beyond our control. We suffer our passions and our attempts to contain them. We submit our passions to our control instead of submitting to them. Nietzsche's treatment of passion is most promising, as he suggests possibilities for allowing passion to remain in productive tension with reason and with other elements in thought and action.

Public and Private. Also bound up with discussions of the body, and of reason and passion, is distinction between the public and the private. All four thinkers variously associate the body and passions with privacy, concealment, singularity, opacity, and inaccessibility. Identity and individuality are understood to be manifest in public but sustained by sources that are in part private. This is especially so for Arendt, for whom the public is the domain of the visible, the common, and appearance, whereas the private is that of the hidden, the singular, and concealment. For Arendt, bodily matters are best kept private, and she joins Nietzsche in suggesting that they may be *necessarily* private, that some aspects of bodily experience possess an opacity and singularity that limit their public expression.

Taylor views the public as the domain of the articulable and of intersubjective reason and the private as the domain of that less amenable to articulation and reason. Arendt and Taylor distinguish the public and private horizontally, in terms of spheres or zones, and all four thinkers distinguish them vertically, in terms of levels of depth and accessibility. To the extent that politics is defined in terms of the public and the body is associated with the private, discussion of politics and the body is inherently difficult.

Reflection and Judgment. Finally, concern with reason and passion, publicity and privacy, and levels of depth and accessibility underlies discussions of reflection and judgment. Although most subdued in Arendt, reflection and judgment are understood by these thinkers to proceed at levels varyingly intense, complex, intelligible, and articulable. Each acknowledges the feelings, moods, dispositions, inclinations, and visceral reactions that are not entirely amenable to representation, articulation, reason, or consciousness. As such, thinking is not restricted to these domains but includes elements of experience outside of them. *Thoughtfulness* requires attention to such elements in thinking. By giving little attention to them, Arendt risks cultivating thoughtlessness. Taylor attends to these elements while failing to appreciate the extent to which, and the varying means by which, they can be modified. Nietzsche and Hampshire emphasize, more challengingly, the extent to which thinking includes these elements and involves techniques of intervention and tactics of experimentation and cultivation.

A theme encountered frequently in discussions of corporeality is that corporeality is inherently difficult to discuss. Because bodily experience is significantly characterized by privacy and opacity, as it often eludes intelligibility and resists representation, attempts to *theorize* corporeality encounter special challenges. Moreover, the very terms of discussion—those listed above, and even more basic terms such as body, mind, thought, and action—are indispensable but also insufficient and problematical. The most profound discussions of corporeality appreciate this, employing such terms while emphasizing their inadequacy and instability, beginning with such terms and then struggling to unsettle and exceed them. One means of doing so, encountered most frequently in Nietzsche and which I pursue myself, is to introduce dissonant formulations—such as "the corporeality of thought"—that unsettle familiar distinctions and stretch our conceptual vocabulary.

Moreover, "the body" mutates across the chapters to follow. For any thinker, the body is a relative term, as it is defined in relation to notions such as consciousness, language, and culture, whose construal affects that of the body. In this respect, the body is often a site of difference; that which exceeds other notions, or is seen as antithetical to them, is relegated to "body." The body becomes a repository for the remainders from other concepts, and the purity of these concepts rests on the impurity of the body.

Thus the body receives attention, if only indirectly or negatively, and inhabits our thinking.

I have introduced my concerns mainly in abstract terms and treat them in this manner in much of what follows. However, as I discuss, examples often have an affective power that stimulates thinking in a way that theoretical statements do not. For this reason, I rely on many examples—actual, hypothetical, and literary—to make vivid and add flesh to my claims. Many of my examples involve sexuality, such as gender reassignment, sexual appetite, racialized desire, and the rehabilitation of sexual offenders. Focusing my examples adds continuity to the discussion, and sexuality is a domain of experience in which there is much current interest.

In the pages to follow I bring into focus the most pressing and promising issues involved in corporeality and politics, exploring their connections and conveying the consequences of their neglect. Such attention to the particularities of the body can rise to theoretical reflection—illuminating, clarifying, probing, undermining, reconfiguring, and reevaluating that which is commonly assumed, neglected, or disparaged. This allows us to advance from implicit materialism, which is increasingly prevalent today, to what Hampshire terms "self-conscious materialism"—a mode of embodiment constantly modified by reflection. By adopting self-conscious materialism, political theorists may not only grasp corporeality and politics but also enter into and transform them. This is a major step toward what Nietzsche claims dispensing with the "soul" requires: coming to grips, finally, with human bodiliness.

NOTES

1. Arthur Kleinman and Joan Kleinman, "How Bodies Remember: Social Memory and Bodily Experience of Criticism, Resistance, and Delegitimation following China's Cultural Revolution," *New Literary History* 25 (1994): 707–23.

2. Gabriel Almond and Sidney Verba, *The Civic Culture* (Boston: Little, Brown, 1965), 104–13, 354–56. Interest in the body is also displayed in James Q. Wilson and Richard J. Hernstein, *Crime and Human Nature* (New York: Simon & Schuster, 1985).

3. See Stanley Cavell, *The Pitch of Philosophy: Autobiographical Exercises* (Cambridge: Harvard University Press, 1994), 87; Jean Cohen, "Democracy, Difference,

and the Right to Privacy," in *Democracy and Difference: Contesting the Boundaries of the Political*, ed. Seyla Benhabib (Princeton: Princeton University Press, 1996), 187–217; William E. Connolly, "A Critique of Pure Politics," *Philosophy and Social Criticism* 23, no. 5 (1997): 1–26; Jean Bethke Elshtain, "Introduction: Bodies and Politics," in *Politics and the Human Body: An Assault on Dignity*, ed. Jean Bethke Elshtain and J. Timothy Cloyd (Nashville: Vanderbilt University Press, 1995), ix–xvi; Martha Nussbaum, "Non-Relative Virtues: An Aristotelian Approach," in *The Quality of Life*, ed. Martha Nussbaum and Amartya Sen (Oxford: Clarendon Press, 1993), 242–69; Hilary Putnam, "How Old Is the Mind? " in *Words and Life*, ed. James Conant (Cambridge: Cambridge University Press, 1994), 3–19; Bernard Williams, *Shame and Necessity* (Berkeley and Los Angeles: University of California Press, 1993), 23–26; and Iris Marion Young, "Communication and the Other: Beyond Deliberative Democracy," in *Democracy and Difference*, 120–35. Connolly and Nussbaum have given the body the most attention; in chapters to follow I note my affinities to the former and differences from the latter.

4.   Valuable contributions include Rosemary Garland Thomson, ed., *Freakery: Cultural Spectacles of the Extraordinary Body* (New York: New York University Press, 1996); Talal Asad, *Genealogies of Religion: Discipline and Reasons of Power in Christianity and Islam* (Baltimore: Johns Hopkins University Press, 1993); Elizabeth Grosz, *Volatile Bodies: Toward a Corporeal Feminism* (Bloomington: Indiana University Press, 1994); Thomas Lacquer, *Making Sex: Body and Gender from the Greeks to Freud* (Cambridge: Harvard University Press, 1990); Alan Hyde, *Bodies of Law* (Princeton: Princeton University Press, 1997); Elaine Scarry, *The Body in Pain: The Making and Unmaking of the World* (New York: Oxford University Press, 1985); Jose Luis Bermudez, Anthony Marcel, and Naomi Eilan, eds., *The Body and the Self* (Cambridge: MIT Press, 1995); Paul Connerton, *How Societies Remember* (Cambridge: Cambridge University Press, 1989).

5.   Richard Sennett remarks that "the body is missing" in recent putative discussions of the body and that many of these discussions, ironically, come across as cold and even puritanical. Richard Sennett, "The Social Body," *Transition* 6, no. 3 (71): 80–98.

6.   See Judith Butler and William Connolly, "Politics, Power, and Ethics: A Discussion," *Theory and Event* 4, 2 (2000): 1–18. The focus on representation is modified slightly in Butler's recent work. Compare *Gender Trouble: Feminism and the Subversion of Identity* (New York: Routledge, 1990) to *The Psychic Life of Power: Theories in Subjection* (Stanford: Stanford University Press, 1997).

7.   Friedrich Nietzsche, *The Gay Science*, trans. Walter Kaufmann (New York: Vintage, 1974), 34–35. The phrase "linguistic turn" appeared first, to my knowledge, in Richard Rorty, ed., *The Linguistic Turn* (Chicago: University of Chicago Press, 1967). For Rorty's reading of Nietzsche (e.g., "[I]n a Nietzschean view . . . to change how we talk is to change what, for our own purposes, we are" [20]) see *Contingency, Irony, and*

Solidarity (Cambridge: Cambridge University Press, 1989). I discuss Rorty's linguistic turn—and in doing so overlook corporeality myself—in John Tambornino, "Philosophy as the Mirror of Liberalism: The Politics of Richard Rorty," *Polity* 30, no. 1 (Fall 1997): 57–78.

1

LOCATING THE BODY

CORPOREALITY AND POLITICS IN HANNAH ARENDT

> The body . . . is the only thing one could not share even if one wanted to.
> Nothing . . . is less common and less communicable, and therefore more
> securely shielded against the visibility and audibility of the public realm.
> . . . Nothing . . . ejects one more radically from the world.
>
> —Hannah Arendt

Many political theorists ignore the body, but Arendt is not one of them. She is powerfully aware of the body, believing that it demands attention—*circumscribed* attention—and seeking a position between those who ignore the body and those who privilege it. Yet her position, which she realizes to be insecure, is ultimately untenable. Her position is that the body does not so much contribute to politics as threaten it. Arendt's location of the body invites this, and her characterizations of the body and of politics entail this.

Despite its limitations, Arendt's treatment of the body helps to identify fundamental issues regarding corporeality and politics. Arendt is instructive on these matters, since her philosophical and political views are often formulated with reference to the body, helping to identify issues and problems. It is because Arendt was intensely aware of the body—even though ambivalent and in places hostile toward it—that she serves as a point of departure for sharpening issues and proceeding in a different direction. Moreover, a more affirmative orientation to the body need not detract from her thought but rather may enrich it. The body, as at moments Arendt suggests, may provide the resources she most cherishes, those that contribute to thinking and acting.

Arendt refers to the body frequently, though usually in order to discuss matters viewed as antithetical to it. Rather than sustained discussion of the body she offers numerous asides. With some exceptions, the body is said to epitomize brute need, enslaving necessity, unrelieved homogeneity, and radical privacy. In addition to her explicit references, Arendt frequently uses terms that, though not always defined or explained, connote the body, such as natality, passion, emotion, sensuousness, mood, feeling, and life.

When our bodies dominate our concerns, we are in essence slaves. Of course, the freest man is still pestered by bodily demands, but he has successfully relegated them to the realm of the private, or at least to that of the social. Given the preciousness of the political, the citizen will limit concern for the body in public life. Yet Arendt's wish that our lives not be dominated by bodily concerns never leads her to envisage liberation from them. To the contrary, she is profoundly aware that the basic demands of life cannot be forgotten, that "there is no lasting happiness outside the prescribed cycle of painful exhaustion and pleasurable regeneration."[1] The most basic needs—food, water, and in most climates shelter and clothing—are constant and unremitting. More fundamentally, we are inescapably embodied creatures, and our orientation to the world involves sensual experience and tactile familiarity.

Many of Arendt's admirers do not take issue with her treatment of the body.[2] Those who do so usually couch their discussion in objections to her notion of the social.[3] Recently, sustained discussions of Arendt's treatment of the body have begun to appear.[4] Against the backdrop of these discussions, I explore questions raised but less pursued—the respects in which politics (Arendtian and otherwise) may attend to the body and in which the body (even the Arendtian body) may contribute to politics.

PHILOSOPHY AND POLITICS

Two philosophical conclusions underlie much of Arendt's thinking: that the metaphysical tradition is no longer credible, and that Being exceeds knowing. These conclusions entail that we lack external standards for evaluating human affairs and that we can never be fully at home on Earth (or in flight from it) or united with one another. At best, our predicament can be partially alleviated by political action—words and deeds that establish durable institutions and provide moments of commonality. In the past two centuries, Arendt contends, the political implications of this philosophical predicament have been disastrously ignored.

As early as her doctoral dissertation Arendt explored the reemergence of the metaphysical tradition in Christianity, in which the earthly and mortal is dwarfed by the spiritual and eternal.[5] Her subsequent writings emphasize how the metaphysical tradition, beginning with Parmenides and continuing at least through Hegel, encouraged humans to give priority not to the worldly realm of objects and action but to the transcendental realm of ideals and thought. This tradition dreamt of "a timeless, spaceless, suprasensuous realm as the proper region of thought."[6] Such dreams followed the frustration and disappointments inherent in politics, leading to its abandonment in search of the harmony, perfection, and eternity it can never provide. The most extreme formulation of this division appeared in the figure of the philosopher-king, representing "the domination of human affairs by something outside its own realm" (WA, 114). Arendt emphasizes the significance of the loss of "Plato's invisible spiritual yardsticks, by which the visible, concrete affairs of men were to be measured and judged" (WA, 127). Without such yardsticks, there is no standpoint outside of human affairs allowing its appraisal or evaluation. Instead, we answer only to ourselves.[7]

Arendt argues that we moderns must acknowledge that nature is without design and will remain, even with advances in science, alien to us.[8] Accepting this is not easy. Indeed, that thought and Being are identical is something that the metaphysical tradition never dared to doubt. Nevertheless, we must reject this assumption and realize that "man is compelled to assent to a Being which he has never created and to which he is essentially alien" (WEP, 37). As thinkers, our task is no longer to discover the *essence* of Being and of ourselves. Rather, we should accept what Arendt believes to be Karl Jaspers's most important lesson:

> Being as such is not knowable, it is to be experienced only as something 'surrounding' us. Thus the very ancient search for an ontology is liquidated. . . . Instead . . . 'the discordance of Being' can be admitted; . . . as well as the modern will to create a human world which can be home within a world which is no

longer a home. It is as if with this concept of Being as that which 'surrounds' us in some fluid contour there were traced an island, on which Man, unmenaced by the dark Unknowable . . . can freely rule and choose. (WEP, 55)

Our predicament—that, for each individual, objects and others remain in some respects alien, with consciousness groping murkily to comprehend them—suggests a new philosophical orientation and political project. It suggests that we should reconcile ourselves to beginning as homeless in the world and join others in constructing and maintaining a reasonably secure home.[9]

Objects are made more familiar through metaphor and imagination. Metaphor allows the unfamiliar to be grasped in terms of the familiar, it is "the human way of *appropriating* and, as it were, disalienating the world into which . . . each of us is born as a newcomer and a stranger" (*LM:T,* 100). Metaphor and imagination are employed in our contact with others, who retain a degree of opacity despite our wish for their familiarity.[10] Being, then, while exceeding consciousness and representation, and never identical to thought, endlessly provokes and challenges us. Arendt contends that the task of thinking is not to reduce Being to the "thinkable" but instead may be, following Jaspers, "'to aggravate . . . [its] unthinkability'" (WEP, 54). Such acknowledgment of the unthinkability of Being enters, at points, Arendt's thinking about the body. At these points, the body's unthinkability allows it to provoke and challenge thinking and to inspire and guide action.

Many are reluctant to accept such estrangement from Being. Indeed, we continue to observe "outbursts of passionate exasperation with reason, thought, and rational discourse which are the natural reactions of men who know from their experiences that thought and reality have parted company."[11] Responding to this estrangement with anger and frustration, or with futile philosophical or political attempts to wholly overcome it, is precisely what Arendt seeks to avoid (WEP, 34–39). Instead, as we shall see, she hopes for a common world—an island of shared language, common sense, public spaces, and concerted action—providing a reprieve from the unthinkability of Being, mysterious and hostile nature, ineffable regions of the self, and our very bodies.

THE PUBLIC AND THE PRIVATE

Arendt's political commitments map her philosophical conclusions. In these, the body is variously present, though seldom as an esteemed constituent or equal participant. Arendt's distinction between the public and the private is often seen as rigid and unyielding. Ideally, the public realm is the realm of freedom, in which persons liberated from the dreary demands of necessity have the opportunity to speak and act, to be political. The public realm cannot, however, dispense with the private. Rather, it depends crucially on the private, requiring that the demands of life, especially those that are most basic and unending, be met:

> The distinctive trait of the household sphere was that in it men lived together because they were driven by their wants and needs. The driving force was life itself. . . . The realm of the *polis,* on the contrary, was the sphere of freedom, and if there was a relationship between these two spheres, . . . mastering of the necessities of life in the household was the condition for freedom of the *polis.* (*HC,* 30–31)

In Athenian democracy, this division required that a portion of the society (i.e., women, slaves, and metics) perform essential tasks, thereby allowing citizens the leisure needed for politics. In societies without such a caste system, a vibrant public realm nonetheless requires that some portion of the population—or of each citizen—meet basic needs and be occupied with nonpolitical concerns, thereby setting aside a space not affected by the demands of daily living (*HC,* 50–58, 72). The brilliance of the American Revolution is said to be its avoidance of social questions and basic needs; the massive error of the French Revolution was its devotion of the public realm to bodily necessity (*OR,* 59–60).

Arendt does not, however, imagine politics and the public realm as having a ghostly emptiness or as populated by disembodied minds. To the contrary, our lives are framed by birth and death and structured by the rhythm of nature (*HC,* 8). The shared world is crucially material, comprised in part by the artifice that *Homo faber* constructs for our mental and bodily orientation. It is the loss of such embodied orientation that underlies Arendt's weariness toward (at least the connotations of) space travel, in which humans float free from the world of human artifice (*HC,* 1–2), and toward the replacement of work by automated labor, in which durable objects to be used are replaced by goods to be consumed (*HC,* 94).

Arendt clings to her particular configuration of the public and private, placing constraints on what is assigned to each realm and contending that "each human activity points to its proper location in the world" (*HC,* 73). She provides a series of distinctions tracking her configuration, such as freedom and necessity, politics and the prepolitical, equality and inequality, nonrule and rule, honor and shame, permanence and futility, displayed and hidden, and visible and invisible. There once was a time in which the body was confined to the second term in each of these pairs, but in the confusion of modernity—"an age which no longer believes that bodily functions and material concerns should be hidden"—it occupies both (*HC,* 73). Indeed, the few remnants of strict privacy today relate to necessities of the body.

Despite its centrality to her work, Arendt concedes that the particular configuration of the public and private, or content of each realm, is not what is most important. Toward the end of her life, when questioned directly by Mary McCarthy as to the content of politics, Arendt responded: "At all times people living together will have affairs that belong in the realm of the public—'are worthy to be talked about in public.' What these matters *are* at any historical *moment* is probably *utterly* different."[12] Rather, what is most important is that there *be* a distinction, that the political be distinguished from the private or nonpolitical. To naturalize any particular distinction between the public and private would be antipolitical, as would erasing the distinction and making everything political. The former stifles politics. The latter starves it.

Arendt's greatest worry, then, is not the particular content of politics today but the prospect that the "gulf" between the private and public has disappeared, that "the two realms . . . constantly flow into each other" (*HC,* 33). The danger of the social stems not only from its introduction of concerns of living into politics and its replacement of action with behavior but also from its threat to the private realm, and by this its threat to the public (*HC,* 45, 47). My concern, then, is less with Arendt's preferences regarding the *content* of politics (a continuing mystery to her readers) than with her insights into the *preparation* for, and *sustenance* of, politics.[13]

This points to a more fundamental, and more interesting, distinction between the public and the private. The private realm can be understood not only *horizontally*, in the spatial sense of a zone or location outside the public realm, but also *vertically*, as that which is beneath the surface or deeply submerged, and *numerically*, as comprised of that which is singular and individual. These latter senses of the private concur with her definition of the public as that which is seen and heard by all, held in common, and shared (*HC,* 50–52). These latter, more fundamental senses of the private are epitomized by the body, as "nothing . . . is less common and less communicable, and therefore more securely shielded against the visibility and audibility of the public realm, than what goes on within the confines of the body" (*HC,* 112).

Similarly, Arendt draws attention to "the veritable gulf that separates all bodily sensations, pleasure or pain, desires and satisfaction—which are so 'private' that they cannot even be adequately voiced, much less represented in the outside world" from mental images, which can be voiced and represented (*HC,* 141). Our bodily sensations are by their nature radically private and are transformed and "deindividualized" when they are given voice and represented in the world (*HC,* 50). In this respect, there is a permanent gulf between the public and the private, with residual privacy nourishing and resisting publicity.

Indeed, hedonism—which maintains that only one's bodily sensations are real—is "the most radical form of a non-political, totally private way of life" (*HC,* 112–13). Arendt does not think highly of such ways of life. And for those not choosing such lives, for individuals who desire a public life of appearance and commonality, a wholly private life is intolerable and allows the greatest suffering to occur. The most intense feelings—those of great bodily pain—are "the most private and least communicable of all," crowding out other experiences and depriving us of a sense of reality, isolating us in our feeling that others do not know what we are experiencing (*HC,* 50–51).

Arendt's position is suggested in literary theorist Elaine Scarry's book *The Body in Pain: The Making and Unmaking of the World,*[14] which brilliantly explores the political significance of pain. Scarry argues that torture strives to induce pain so intense and inexpressible as to isolate individuals—alienating them from their language and values, removing them from the common world, and reducing them to a prelinguistic state of noises and cries. Intense, prolonged pain obliterates the common world, it is "language-destroying" and "world-destroying" (29, 35). Moreover, one of the consequences of torture is "an almost obscene conflation of private and public. It brings with it all the solitude of absolute privacy with none of its safety, all the self-exposure of the utterly public with none of its possibility for camaraderie or shared experience" (55). This concurs with Arendt's belief that, absent a common world, bodily experience possesses a "cruel privacy" (*HC*, 117). Similarly, Richard Rorty illuminates an important dimension of social movements, such as feminism, that seek to make suffering less individual and private, to provide language allowing isolated individuals to make sense of their experiences and injuries, which previously were felt to be theirs alone.[15]

Although continual effort is needed to maintain a common world and public realm (which Arendt believed to be in shoddy form in her day), these cannot and should not supplant the private. Rather, a delicate balance must be maintained between the private and the public, between that remaining in the shadows and that exposed to bright light. Whereas total isolation makes the self meaningless, total publicity destroys it (WEP, 49). This is why, despite her love for, and privileging of, the public realm, Arendt can state, with tension but not contradiction, that a "life spent entirely in public" would be "shallow" (*HC*, 71). It is also why she believed that when everything becomes political and privacy is eliminated, a society is on the verge of totalitarianism, as freedom and individuality are made impossible.

Czech novelist Milan Kundera, who shares many of Arendt's philosophical and political influences, echoes her when portraying the public realm, especially in totalitarian but also in liberal capitalist societies, as monotonous, regimented, conformist, and shallow. Yet Kundera's response differs from Arendt's, as he locates opportunities for initiation and individuality in private, sensual relations, viewing the private realm as allowing endless possibilities for shared experiences among otherwise isolated persons. Clandestine encounters and private relations are viewed as havens that sustain individuals, enabling them to endure the banalities of public life, to experience profundity amid shallowness, to interrupt the familiar and the routine. Kundera thus provides an alternative course for those confronted by barren public realms. He has, for his part, moved toward Arendt's position, creating characters whose private relations enable them to care about the common world (by pretending that the world is populated by intimates about whom they care the most) and for whom the richness of the common world sustains their private relations.[16] For Arendt, however, natality and freedom are more exceptional phenomena that appear, when they do, in public.

NATALITY AND FREEDOM

For Arendt, natality and freedom, spontaneity and initiative are not merely incidental features of the human condition. Rather, we are "being[s] whose essence is beginning."[17] Politics and the public realm provide the space for natality and freedom. The private realm—especially the depths and opacities of the self—provides their sources. As with the public realm, made distinct in contrast to the private, freedom is only discernible in contrast to necessity (*HC*, 71). Being liberated from necessity does not, by itself, make us free but only gives us *the opportunity* to be free. A fundamental mistake of the French Revolution and of Marxism is said to have been the belief that freedom consisted solely in eliminating necessity.

When confronted with natality and freedom—the "treasures" with which humans have been gifted—Arendt often settles for *supra*physical explanations. That is, she imagines their sources to be irreducible to one's physicality and their manifestation to exceed it. Arendt's discussions of natality—"the central category of political thought" (*HC*, 9)—are not always clear and never conclusive. This is so because the topic itself does not allow clarity and conclusiveness. She often speaks of natality in the literal sense, of new humans constantly arriving in the world. Each birth is a new beginning, in that a unique human being enters the world and responds to it through initiative. Such initiative is portrayed as a "second birth," in which humans "insert" themselves into the world through words and deeds (*HC*, 176–77). The final page of *The Life of the Mind* concludes (candid in its uncertainty) that the simple fact of new generations may suffice to explain new beginnings, that "the very capacity for beginning is rooted in *natality,* and by no means in creativity, not in a gift but in the fact that human beings, new men, again and again appear in the world by virtue of birth." Arendt realizes that this "seems to tell us no more than that we are *doomed* to be free by virtue of being born."[18]

However, throughout her earlier writings, Arendt resists this conclusion, seeing the "capacity to begin" as "a supreme gift which only man . . . seems to have received" and its manifestation in public as by no means guaranteed.[19] The sources of action are said to be elusive and hidden, and their public manifestation exceptional rather than automatic. In such discussions, Arendt explains the unforeseen, the unexpected, the unprecedented—indeed, the inexplicable—by recourse to the miraculous:

> Every act . . . is a 'miracle'—that is, something which could not be expected. If it is true that action and beginning are essentially the same, it follows that a capacity for performing miracles must likewise be within the range of human faculties. This sounds stranger than it actually is. (WF, 169)

Arendt suggests that her use of the term miracle is largely figurative, but it is so because it is her stopping point, beyond which she cannot speak adequately. The miraculous gestures toward a *fugitive* realm, prior to and partially eluding language, thinking, and action, which nourishes their innovation.[20]

Freedom, breaking from the routine and ordinary to introduce the novel and extraordinary, draws on this fugitive realm. In societies without a public realm, without opportunities for appearance and action, these sources of freedom remain untapped. And if these sources are eliminated—extinguished, domesticated, or so illuminated as to be no longer mysterious—then the public world of freedom and beginnings will itself be barren and uncreative. While natality and freedom are political, manifest in public as a "worldly, tangible reality" (WF, 169), their sources are importantly prepolitical and private.

An actual instance of Arendt's intimations of the submerged, prepolitical sources for political action appears in George Chauncey's fascinating *Gay New York: Gender, Urban Culture, and the Making of the Gay Male World,*

1890–1940.[21] Chauncey details the extensive, fugitive social and sexual underworld of homosexual men, which eventually accumulated the energy and solidity needed to burst above ground as a new political presence, claiming public space and recognition. Contrary to Arendt's emphases, however, this emergence was importantly inspired by bodily dispositions and involved politicizing the needs, uses, and possibilities of the body. Indeed, recent lesbian and gay politics has often had a public, performative, disruptive quality (such as ACT UP demonstrations and staged "kiss-ins"), making use of dramatic displays intended to have somatic effects, in order to politicize highly personal, traditionally private matters.[22]

Arendt's distinction between prepolitical sources for freedom and opportunities for their political manifestation sheds light on her distinction between ancient and modern freedom and on her treatment of the will. Woven into Arendt's discussions of natality and freedom are references to the will, a faculty toward which she was ambivalent. She laments its introduction to post-Roman political thought and applauds the American founders for "bypassing . . . [this] trickiest and . . . most dangerous of modern concepts and misconceptions" (*OR*, 225). Essentially, she sees the will as pivotal in the substitution of philosophical for political freedom. Whereas the ancients' political freedom consisted of concerted action, modern philosophical freedom is said to require only an individual state of mind (WF, 144–46). Moreover, many conceptions of the will serve what Arendt believes to be the misguided ideal of sovereign self-mastery, in which we strive for full control of our actions and identity by commanding subordinate elements in society and in ourselves.[23]

However, in her final writings Arendt emphasizes the importance of the will, contending that it was not invented but *discovered* and may be necessary to account for natality and freedom (*LM:W*, 69). Yet the will is viewed as a mysterious faculty, its existence assumed rather than proven (*LM:W*, 32, 89). In her conception, the will is independent of reason and desire and distinct from thinking and judging (*LM:W*, 69). Above all, the will is a "mental organ" of freedom and spontaneity, freeing us from the necessity (whether logical, historical, or bodily) that Arendt so abhors (*LM:W*, 110). Importantly, Arendt remains true to a feature of the will present in many of its past formulations: that it alleviates the monotony and limits of our bodies, freeing us from the strictures of our mere physicality by overcoming the body's resistance (*LM:W,* 70–71). In doing so, she adopts the past tendency to depreciate the body.

Whether or not conceived in terms of the will, for Arendt initiative is conceived as a *transcendence* of mere physicality. The will, the opacities of the self, and (a perhaps merely figurative notion of) miracles account for the blessed mystery of inspiration, of individuals taking the initiative to be something no person has ever been and groups daring to do things never before done (*LM:W,* 3–7). Arendt assumes that the body contributes little to such inspiration and beginnings, an assumption repeated in her conception of the role of the body in selfhood and identity and of the body's defining attributes—need, passion, desire, and feeling—in thinking and judging. Instead, selfhood and identity, thinking and judging draw little from the body and are, in crucial respects, defined in opposition to it.

THE BODY AND THE SELF

Discussion of the inchoate sources for natality and freedom and of the depths fueling language, thinking, and acting leads us to Arendt's position regarding the role of the body in selfhood and public appearance. Piecing together her conceptions of these helps to identify her assumptions regarding the body.

Arendt speaks of the self as that which unites the body, soul, and mind, with the body and soul more closely associated than either is with the mind (*LM:W,* 4, 31). The activities of the mind are thinking, willing, and judging, which occur in the medium of language. Whereas the contents of the mind can be expressed without inherent difficulty, the dispositions of the body and soul, owing to their intensity and interiority and their priority to language, remain hidden, never adequately expressed or fully apparent. Expression of attributes of the body and soul—dispositions, feelings, passions, emotions— is mediated by thought and reflection. Mediation by thought and translation into speech *individualizes* these attributes. Although the body may "prompt" us toward certain utterances or actions, we "decide what is fit to appear" (*LM:T,* 31–32). It is because of this needed step of the mind (some combination of thinking, willing, and judging) that "a mindless creature cannot possess . . . personal identity; it is at the complete mercy of its inner life process, its moods and emotions" (*LM:T,* 32).

Given the constraints of physical makeup and abilities, we choose our words and deeds and how we wish to appear, "*[u]p to a point*" (*LM:T,* 34). This outward appearance is not simply a manifestation of inner disposition. If it were, given the near sameness of our bodies and dispositions, we would tend to speak and act alike. That is, the "monotonous sameness and pervasive ugliness" of inner dispositions, contrasted with the "enormous variety and richness of overt human conduct, witness to the radical difference between the inside and outside of the human body" (*LM:T,* 35). For example, Arendt explains, although the sexual urge, rooted in the reproductive organs, is basically the same across individuals, every manifestation of love is unique (*LM:T,* 35).[24]

We do not, then, alter our inner dispositions so much as display or hide them, choosing what is "fit" to appear by concealing some things and revealing others (*LM:T,* 21, 29–35). Courage, for example, consists not in eliminating our fears but in deciding not to show them (*LM:T,* 36). Rarely does our public appearance or self-presentation correspond fully to our inner dispositions. This is because our appearance is seldom true to all of our conflicting inner dispositions; the former is at best a selection and translation of the latter.[25] For this reason, the potential for hypocrisy and pretense—presenting ourselves as other than we "really" are—is inherent in public appearance. Attempts to hold persons to appearances that truly reflect their inner life lead to assertions of their failure to do so. This is why, in the French Revolution, the demand that individuals confirm the innermost motives behind their principles and actions led to uncertainty, suspicion, and accusations of hypocrisy. A politics requiring such confirmation "poison[s]" our relations and makes suspects of us all (*OR,* 98).[26]

Rather, the standard we should be held to in public appearance is consistency and duration, culminating in character or personality, a "comprehensible and readily identifiable whole" (*LM:T,* 37). The strength of Arendt's position becomes apparent when contrasted with recent discussions of sexual identity. These discussions have become entrenched in an opposition between "biological determinists," who see expressions of sexuality (e.g., "gay") as corresponding to one's true, genetically inherited makeup, and "social constructionists," who see such expressions as wholly contingent, bearing no necessary relation to inherited makeup or inner dispositions.[27] Arendt's position alleviates this unsatisfying stalemate. Borrowing from her, to identify oneself as gay is, following inner "promptings," to say that *some of* one's most strongly felt dispositions have been translated—usually imperfectly, given the linguistic and cultural terms available—into a stable presentation to others. For such individuals to present themselves as heterosexual would "hide or disfigure" these dispositions (*LM:T,* 21). Again, when presenting ourselves we exercise choice, but only *"up to a point."*

Within these discussions of individuality and self-presentation, we find one strand of Arendt's view of the body. This is her tendency to view bodies as largely homogeneous and undifferentiated, and consequently contributing little to individuality. This view is exhibited in such statements as "no matter how different and individualized we appear and how deliberately we have chosen this individuality—it always remains true that 'inside we're all alike' " (*LM:T,* 37). That the body is undifferentiated, uninteresting, and unattractive is conveyed in (rather odd) passages such as the following:

> Inside organs, . . . contrary [to external features] are never pleasing to the eye; once forced into view, they look as though they had been thrown together piecemeal and, unless deformed by disease or some peculiar abnormality, they appear alike; not even the various animal species, let alone the individuals, are easy to tell from each other by the mere inspection of their intestines. (*LM:T,* 29)

Given Arendt's assumption of inner similarity and her observation of outward variety, she is led to conclude—in tension with her discussions of the opacity of the self as a source for natality and freedom—that "our common conviction that what is inside ourselves, our 'inner life,' is more relevant to what we 'are' than what appears on the outside is an illusion" (*LM:T,* 30). Initiative for individuating appearances, Arendt usually emphasizes, stems not from the body but from the will.

Arendt's emphasis on the homogeneity of bodies and the immutability of inner dispositions coincides with her emphasis on the body's predictable and unrelenting needs, needs that can be so enslaving as to hinder political action. One of the three principal human activities, labor, corresponds to the body's basic biological processes (*HC,* 7). For this reason, unlike the two other principal human activities, action and work, labor is fundamentally antipolitical, since "man is neither together with the world nor with other people, but alone with his body, facing the naked necessity to keep himself alive" (*HC,* 212). Moreover, given the essential sameness of human bodies, the "somatic experience" of laboring together unites us, in the very rhythms of our bodies, to the point that we cease to be individuals (*HC,* 214).

Free acts are those that could have been left undone, whereas desire and appetite are often felt with such force as to place us under compulsion, overriding will or reason (*LM:W,* 5). As with individuating appearances, action hinges—as it *must,* once the body has been defined in terms of necessity—upon the will. The French Revolution is for Arendt a frightening demonstration of the tyranny of bodies, of political agendas and morality itself corrupted by the privileging of bodily needs and the reliance on physical impulse. Needs can make themselves felt with such urgency as to invade the realm of politics and freedom, as when "the poor, driven by the needs of their bodies, burst on to the scene" *(OR,* 59). The result in that instance was terror. The needs of life trumped freedom, and reason and the political were overwhelmed by a dangerous element in the citizenry. Its reign destroyed freedom.[28]

There is, however, another strand in Arendt's thought that emphasizes not the brute immutability of the body but the extent to which it is altered and conditioned by society. Humans have always been "conditioned beings," as we are changed by the world we create, but the pace and very workings of life, including the bodies of subjects, have been altered dramatically by the tempo of modernity. In the modern era, science and technology, even through seemingly innocuous inventions such as the wristwatch, have "changed the whole rhythm and very physiognomy of human life" (*HC,* 289). And yet, despite the reach of such conditioning and the extent to which we are reconstituted by forces of nature and society, Arendt once again maintains her conviction that "the conditions of human existence . . . *never condition us absolutely*" (*HC,* 11, emphasis mine). Instead, there is believed to be some aspect of each individual, some remote, durable core, immune to such conditioning.

In her discussion of the education of children, Arendt suggests that the child, unmistakably embodied and rapidly developing, is fairly receptive to socialization, "not finished but in a state of becoming."[29] Education plays the crucial political role of introducing newcomers to the world by inculcating certain beliefs, values, and habits (CE, 175). Given the uniqueness of each child and the alien quality of the world, the child must be "gradually introduced" to it, and "care must be taken that this new thing comes to fruition in relation to the world as it is" (CE, 189). Arendt acknowledges that early education requires a certain amount of uniformity, drill, and repetition. But education must balance delicately the newness of each individual with the need to introduce him or her to the common world, thereby allowing individual initiative while ensuring the world's survival. Continuous with my reading of Arendt, the sources of individuality are assumed, without specification, to reside beyond the common world, never entirely encroached upon by it.[30]

Given such emphases on the entanglement and interpenetration of the common world and the body, it would seem that concern for the former would necessitate concern for the latter. Yet this is not Arendt's course. Instead of being drawn toward the body, she is drawn away, defining thinking and politics in opposition to it. When she is emphasizing the uniformity and immutability of the body, her inattention may be tenable. But her other emphases, which acknowledge the entanglement of the body and the common world, make her inattention far less viable.

THINKING AND JUDGING

The two remaining topics, thinking and judging, are especially difficult to reconstruct, in part owing to Arendt's inability to complete her work on judging.[31] My discussion focuses on those aspects of her conceptions most pertinent to the body and the opacities of the self, contending that Arendt's orientation to the body does not enhance her conceptions of thinking and judging but rather limits them. Thinking, along with its antithesis, thoughtlessness, is one of Arendt's most fundamental concerns. She believes that the inability or unwillingness to think is what allows evildoing and that in the contemporary world too infrequently do we "*stop* and think" (*LM:T,* 4). In terms of Arendt's conception of the self, thinking is the province of the mind and occurs in the medium of language. Further, like politics and freedom, thinking is exceptional; it is a departure from the ordinary and from necessity. And as with politics and freedom, thinking is threatened by the demands and distractions of the body and requires temporary relief from them (*LM:T,* 44; *LM:W,* 34).

What occurs when we stop and think? We carry on a conversation with ourselves, attempting to come to agreement. These two characteristics of thinking are relevant to our discussion of the body. First, thinking is portrayed not as a monologue but as a "solitary *dialogue* . . . an intercourse between me and myself."[32] Thinking is a dialogue involving the divergent views we entertain; it is an encounter between competing voices. Thinking, then, involves less the inarticulate regions of the self than the articulate. Second, the outcome of thinking is the elimination of contradictions in oneself—a resolution between disputing voices expressing contrary commitments. It is because we must live with ourselves that we do not want such contradictions.[33]

This is a sophisticated conception of thinking, one that attends to the plurality internal to each of us. However, Arendt appears to construe the plurality internal to thought as restricted to the mind; that is, as involving less the conflict between the mind, body, and soul than conflicts *within* the mind. Moreover, her conception expects too much in terms of internal reconciliation and the overcoming of contradictions, as it assumes that being able to live with oneself requires that we achieve these aims. Yet if we construe thinking as not limited to the mind but as involving the body (which Arendt herself presumes to be often in conflict with the mind), then the hope of eliminating such conflict must be tempered. Not to do so would almost certainly lead to the attempts to subordinate aspects of the self that Arendt herself rejects. Nietzsche and Hampshire, in contrast, *broaden* and *deepen* their respective conceptions of thinking to encompass the plurality internal to each self, and give attention to elements—inchoate, dissonant passions, desires, feelings, moods, and inclinations—that reside *beneath* consciousness and articulation but that are nonetheless part of thinking. Instead of striving for elimination of inner contradictions, each suggests that we accommodate such dissonance, that we not require inner harmony in order to live with ourselves.

Although Arendt did not live to treat judgment fully, as she planned to do in the third volume of *The Life of the Mind*, to be entitled *Judging*, two conclusions on her part are discernible. First, she believes that the application of principles is inherently indeterminate and involves considerable discretion, and that this matters politically. Principles are indeterminate in that their generality prevents neat application in particular circumstances. As a result, there is always a space of discretion between principles and their application. Drawing on Kant (and echoing Wittgenstein), she writes:

> Judgment . . . the mysterious endowment of the mind by which the general, always a mental construction, and the particular, always given to sense experience, are brought together, is a 'peculiar faculty' and in no way inherent in the intellect, not even in the case of 'determinant judgments' . . . because no rule is available for the applications of the rule. (*LM:T,* 69)[34]

Despite the irreducible gap between a principle and its application—a gap never entirely closed by determinate reason or by additional principles—principles are indispensable for evaluation and action.[35] Though never entirely subject to dispute, the *more* principled are evaluation and action, the more they are accessible, thus permitting reasoned debate and criticism.

If the unprincipled, inaccessible elements in thinking and acting become too great, then things can get terribly out of hand. This is said to have occurred in the French Revolution, when reason, in its generality and cold abstractness, was believed to stifle compassion, with its concern for the particularity and immediacy of suffering (*OR,* 85). Arendt fears that compassion is so particular and individual as to be *mute*, not allowing argumentation and compromise. Instead, solidarity is more appropriate than compassion for politics, because it centers on reason and generality, allowing it to more reliably guide evaluation and inspire action (*OR,* 85–89).[36] The problem, then, is that the inaccessible, potentially dangerous elements in thinking and action, which cannot be eliminated since they are needed to supplement principles, must not become too great. Arendt often associates these inaccessible elements with the body, characterizing them as passion or emotion.[37]

This illuminates Arendt's brief remarks on how the formation of opinion requires open discussion and public debate and how without this opportunity we have only "fickle and unreliable" moods (*OR*, 268–69). Indeed, the modern individual, that antipolitical creature whom Arendt held in such low regard, is characterized in part by "his ever-changing moods and the radical subjectivism of his emotional life" (*HC*, 39). In both cases, emotion is insufficiently mediated by discussion, and that which should be private is mistakenly regarded as public.[38]

Similar concerns emerge in a second strand in Arendt's treatment of judgment. Here she emphasizes Kant's distinction between determinate and reflective judgment, identifying the latter as appropriate not only for aesthetic judgment (as it was for Kant) but also for political judgment. In reflective judgment, we begin not with general principles under which the particular is then subsumed but rather with particulars, relying on those identified as "exemplary" to arrive at generalized particulars. In doing so, thought does not remain too particularized (as when compassion reigns) but proceeds from particulars to greater generality.[39] Reflective judgment encourages us to imagine the standpoint of others and to include them in our generalization. To do so is to "go visiting," transcending our immediate, private sensations and making present those beyond our purview, thereby enlarging our thought (*LK*, 42–44).

Yet, like determinate judgment, reflective judgment includes considerable discretion. It must do so, as it requires us to select one of many examples as exemplary and to rely on it to evaluate the rest. For Arendt, this space of discretion must limit the influence of private sensations. Appropriating Kant, she explains:

> [J]udgment must liberate itself from the 'subjective private conditions,' that is, from the idiosyncrasies which naturally determine the outlook of each individual in his privacy and are legitimate as long as they are only privately held opinions, but which are not fit to enter the market place, and lack all validity in the public realm.[40]

In place of private opinions—made up to a considerable extent of private sensations and incommunicable feelings, and little subject to modification—we must cultivate "taste" in order to be capable of judgment (CC, 219). In contrast to sensations and feelings, taste is subject to dispute precisely because it can be made public by communication (CC, 222).[41] Taste is, instead, the product of a "truly cultivated mind" (CC, 224).

Given her appreciation of the social and cultural penetration of the body, there is a basis in Arendt for exploring possibilities for working on and modifying sensations and feelings (and their entwined passions, desires, sentiments, moods, and dispositions) that enter politics. Yet possibilities for work on the self that involve the body play no role in Arendt's politics nor in preparation for such politics.[42] Yet modifying feelings, often through techniques of the self involving the body, can affect thinking and judging and enable acting. A revised Arendtian politics could make feelings an object of political attention and, in order to do so, make bodily activity an aspect of reflection. Not to give the body such attention encourages thoughtlessness.[43]

Although there are countertendencies in her thinking, Arendt's location of the body tends to excise corporeality from politics. Yet words and deeds, artifice and institutions organize the body and are sustained by it. Thus, politics of any substance involves the body. A revised Arendtian politics would make the body a concern and appreciate its contribution to natality and individuality, and attention to the body would be part of political thinking and judging. Such a politics would be attentive to the entire relationship between corporeality and politics—the influence of thinking and acting on the body, and its influence on thinking and acting.

The alternative, seen in Arendt's stricter moments and in some of her admirers, to seek a politics cleanly separated from the concerns of the body and of the social, leads to a dead end. It makes politics an extremely rare, isolated event, while depoliticizing vast domains of life. This gives rise to disappointment over the fact that genuine politics hardly ever occurs in our "apolitical" lives. Furthermore, Arendt is, as her admirers rightly stress, deeply committed to freedom and plurality. But her construal of these is narrowed by her aversion to the body and neglect of crucial dimensions of life.

Arendt's treatment of the body is still illuminating, especially regarding the multiple senses of the public and private; the importance of sources for natality and individuality; the opacities of the self; the role of passion and mood in politics and of private sensations in judgment; and the decision, often political, of what to reveal of oneself and what to conceal. Examining Arendt's treatment of the body helps us understand the politics of the body and Arendt's thinking itself. Indeed, it helps us grasp the cryptic claim with which she concluded her seminal essay "What Is Existenz Philosophy?"— that fundamental to a new definition of human dignity would be recognition that man "is more than any of his thoughts" (56). In pages to follow I consider the extent to which individuals are more than their thoughts and the indignities that result from not recognizing this.

NOTES

1. Hannah Arendt, *The Human Condition* (Chicago: University of Chicago Press, 1958), 108 (hereafter cited *HC*). See also Hannah Arendt, "What Is Authority?" in *Between Past and Future* (New York: Penguin Books, 1954), 117 (hereafter cited WA); and Hannah Arendt, *On Revolution* (New York: Penguin Books, 1963), 59 (hereafter cited *OR*).

2. Dana Villa, in a probing study of Arendt's critique of the metaphysical tradition, conception of the self, theorization of action, and relation to Aristotle, Kant, Nietzsche, and Heidegger, makes no mention of the body. See *Arendt and Heidegger: The Fate of the Political* (Princeton: Princeton University Press, 1996). Mary Dietz, following an impressive critique of Arendt's inattention to gender, asserts "nothing in Arendt's discussion of plurality . . . condemns the literal body (or issues concerning life or the social control of the body) to the sphere of the private realm." Dietz relies on the fact that Arendt often portrays the public realm in terms that may imply the body, such as passion and appearance, while ignoring her explicit treatment of the body. See "Hannah Arendt and Feminist Politics," in *Feminist Interpretations and Political Theory*, ed. Mary Lyndon Shanley and Carole Pateman (Cambridge, England: Polity Press, 1991), 248.

3. Richard Bernstein maintains that Arendt's "categorical distinction between the social and the political is unstable and reveals profound tensions." Richard J. Bernstein, "Rethinking the Social and the Political," in *Philosophical Profiles: Essays in a Pragmatic Mode* (Philadelphia: University of Pennsylvania Press, 1986), 238. See also Hanna Fenichel Pitkin, *The Attack of the Blob: Hannah Arendt's Concept of the Social* (Chicago: University of Chicago Press, 1998).

4. Bonnie Honig argues that for Arendt the "human body is . . . a master signifier of necessity, irresistibility, imitability, and the determination of pure process" and that political action and public identity require us to distinguish ourselves beyond our mere physicality. See "Toward an Agonistic Feminism: Hannah Arendt and the Politics of Identity," in *Feminist Interpretations of Hannah Arendt,* ed. Bonnie Honig (University Park: Pennsylvania State University Press, 1995), 138. Linda M. G. Zerilli elaborates how the body is, for Arendt, uncanny, dangerous, forbidden, sacred, secret, uniform, incommunicable, and a threat to mastery and plurality, thereby conveying the anxiety and terror we feel in regard to our bodies. See "The Arendtian Body," in *Feminist Interpretations,* 167–93.

5. Hannah Arendt, *Love and Saint Augustine,* ed. Joanna Vecchiarelli Scott and Judith Chelius Stark (Chicago: University of Chicago Press, 1996). An excellent discussion of the implications of Augustine's theology for the body and sexuality is found in Peter Brown, *The Body and Society: Men, Women, and Sexual Renunciation in Early Christianity* (New York: Columbia University Press, 1988), 387–427.

6. Arendt, preface to *Between Past and Future,* 11.

7. See also Hannah Arendt, *The Life of the Mind: Thinking* (New York: Harcourt Brace, 1978), 10. Hereafter cited *LM:T.*

8. Hannah Arendt, "What Is Existenz Philosophy?" *Partisan Review* 13, no. 1 (Winter 1946): 34–56. Hereafter cited WEP.

9. A similar conclusion is reached by Bernard Williams: "We are in an ethical condition that lies not only beyond Christianity, but beyond its Kantian and its Hegelian legacies. . . . We know that the world was not made for us, or we for the world, that our history tells no purposive story, and that there is no position outside the world or outside history from which we might hope to authenticate our activities." *Shame and Necessity* (Berkeley and Los Angeles: University of California Press, 1993), 66.

10. Hannah Arendt, "Understanding and Politics," *Partisan Review* 20, no. 4 (1953): 391–92.

11. Arendt, preface to *Between Past and Future,* 6.

12. Quoted in Bernstein, "Rethinking the Social and the Political," 251. See also *HC,* 46–47. Honig, "Toward an Agonistic Feminism," 144–49, argues that, given Arendt's other commitments, any configuration between the public and the private is contingent and unstable and invites contestation.

13. That Arendt values the public over the private (in contrast to liberals, for example, who value the private over the public) need not limit appropriation of her insights.

14. Elaine Scarry, *The Body in Pain: The Making and Unmaking of the World* (New York: Oxford University Press, 1985).

15. See Richard Rorty, "Feminism and Pragmatism," *Michigan Quarterly Review* (1991): 231–58. I discuss Scarry and Rorty in John Tambornino, "Philosophy as the Mirror of Liberalism: The Politics of Richard Rorty," *Polity* 30, no. 1 (Fall 1997): 57–78.

16. See Milan Kundera, *The Book of Laughter and Forgetting*, trans. Michael Henry Heim (New York: Penguin Books, 1980); *The Unbearable Lightness of Being*, trans. Michael Henry Heim (New York: Harper Perennial, 1984); and *Immortality*, trans. Peter Kussi (New York: Harper Perennial, 1992). For the more Arendtian position, see Milan Kundera, *Identity*, trans. Linda Asher (New York: HarperCollins, 1998).

17. Arendt, "Understanding and Politics," 391.

18. Hannah Arendt, *The Life of the Mind: Willing* (New York: Harcourt Brace, 1978), 217. Hereafter cited *LM:W.* This section was first drafted shortly after a scientific breakthrough in cloning sheep and expert consensus that it is possible to clone humans. Whether this undercuts Arendt's assumption of the unforeseeable uniqueness of each human being entering the world, or whether it underscores her emphasis on individuality as comprised chiefly of characteristics attained beyond one's inherited physical makeup, remains to be seen. For discussion of such eventualities, see Martha C. Nussbaum and Cass R. Sunstein, eds., *Clones and Cloning: Facts and Fantasies about Human Cloning* (New York: Norton, 1998).

19. Arendt, "What Is Freedom?" in *Between Past and Future,* 169. Hereafter cited WF.

20. At points, Arendt alludes to the virgin birth of Jesus as the paradigm of miraculous beginnings and unique events (see *OR,* 27; *HC,* 247). Nietzsche suggests that the myth of the virgin birth is a costly inheritance, as it sanitizes creation and views becoming as less bodily than divine. See Friedrich Nietzsche, *Thus Spoke Zarathustra: A Book for None and All,* trans. Walter Kaufmann (New York: Penguin Books, 1978), 261, 291.

21. George Chauncey, *Gay New York: Gender, Urban Culture, and the Making of the Gay Male World, 1890–1940* (New York: Basic Books, 1994).

22. For a perceptive discussion of the distinctive qualities of lesbian and gay identity and politics, which invokes Arendt, see Michael Warner, ed., *Fear of a Queer Planet: Queer Politics and Social Theory* (Minneapolis: University of Minnesota Press, 1993), vii–xxxi.

23. See WF, 163–65; *LM:W,* 161. Williams, *Shame and Necessity,* 29–49, 66–68, argues that the Greeks had, in so many words, a notion of "the will," that is, of individual self-control, deliberation, and action. He concurs with Arendt, however, that the Greeks did not see voluntary action as a philosophical (at least not "metaphysically deepened") problem (68).

24. In formulating the above paragraphs I benefited from Suzanne Duvall Jacobitti, "Thinking about the Self," in *Hannah Arendt: Twenty Years Later,* ed. Larry May and Jerome Kohn (Cambridge: MIT Press, 1996), 199–219.

25. Honig, "Toward an Agonistic Feminism," 142, similarly argues that for Arendt the inner multiplicity of the self is a source of "power and energy" for expression and action.

26. These paragraphs were written before American politics became engulfed in questions of what President Clinton had done in private and, once this was established,

of whether his accounts and apologies were *sincere.* I return to the problem of sincerity in chapter 4.

27. See the symposium "The Science of Homosexuality," *Harvard Gay and Lesbian Review* (Winter 1997): 4, 13–30. For a valuable discussion of Arendt's treatment of sexual identity and of the ways in which her thought in general may contribute to thinking through the politics of sexuality, see Morris B. Kaplan, "Refiguring the Jewish Question: Arendt, Proust, and the Politics of Sexuality," in *Feminist Interpretations of Hannah Arendt,* 105–33.

28. For an account of the French Revolution that discusses the prominence of concern for the body, see Dorinda Outram, *The Body and the French Revolution: Sex, Class, and Political Culture* (New Haven: Yale University Press, 1989).

29. Hannah Arendt, "The Crisis in Education," in *Between Past and Future,* 185. Hereafter cited CE.

30. A similar view of education is expressed in Richard Rorty, "Education without Dogma," *Dissent* (Spring 1989): 198–204. Yet Rorty portrays young persons as more receptive to socialization than does Arendt, assuming them to be thoroughly malleable, possessing little bodily recalcitrance (for him, the troublesome notion of "a true self") that might frustrate such efforts. This portrait stems from his overemphasis on the linguistic and resultant underemphasis on corporeality.

31. Numerous attempts to reconstruct Arendt's theory of judgment have resulted in widely varying characterizations. See Ronald Beiner, "Interpretive Essay," in *Hannah Arendt: Lectures on Kant's Political Philosophy,* ed. Ronald Beiner (Chicago: University of Chicago Press, 1982), 89–156 (hereafter cited *LK*); Seyla Benhabib, *The Reluctant Modernism of Hannah Arendt* (Thousand Oaks, Calif.: Sage, 1996), 173–203; Peter Steinberger, "Arendt on Judgment," *American Journal of Political Science* 34, no. 3 (August 1990): 803–21; and Lisa Jane Disch, *Hannah Arendt and the Limits of Philosophy* (Ithaca: Cornell University Press, 1994).

32. Hannah Arendt, "Thinking and Moral Considerations," *Social Research* 51, no. 1–2 (1984): 35.

33. See Elizabeth Young-Bruehl, *Mind and the Body Politic* (New York: Routledge, 1989), 24–25.

34. Arendt concurs with Wittgenstein's discussion of rule following, which contends that even thinking presumed to be the most formal and determinate may depend on convention, habit, and ineffable inspiration. See Ludwig Wittgenstein, *Philosophical Investigations,* 3d ed., trans. G. E. M. Anscombe (New York: Macmillan, 1958), par. 81–243. A lucid discussion, drawing on Wittgenstein, of the discretion inherent in rule following and, consequently, the permanent chasm between theory and practice is found in Richard E. Flathman, "Theory and Practice, Skepticism and Liberalism," in *Toward a Liberalism* (Ithaca: Cornell University Press, 1989), 14–47.

35. See the related discussion in WF, 152.

36. What would appear to be an antithetical position is found in Martha Nussbaum,

"Compassion: The Basic Social Emotion," *Social Philosophy and Policy* 13, no. 1 (Winter 1996): 27–58. Yet in attempting to allay fears such as those of Arendt that emotions are dangerously irrational and inarticulate, Nussbaum goes to such lengths to assure readers that compassion is rational and cognitive, that it rests on reason and defensible judgments, and that particular bodily feelings need not occur, that when she is done, compassion no longer looks like an *emotion*. It looks like Arendtian solidarity. Nevertheless, Nussbaum maintains that compassion is valuable because it emphasizes human sameness ("essentialism"), which is one of the reasons for Arendt's reservations toward it.

37. George Kateb, *Hannah Arendt: Politics, Conscience, Evil* (Totowa, N.J.: Rowman & Allanhead, 1984), 25–29, argues that Arendt does not necessarily want to exclude all emotion from politics but only certain emotions (e.g., love, goodness, conscience, compassion, pity, and ambition) that she believes threaten politics. Kateb worries, with considerable warrant, that a politics purged of these emotions risks tremendous cruelty.

38. Although space prevents its exploration, Arendt's discussion of common sense (the *sensus communis*) returns us to my earlier discussion of the gulf between the body and the common world. Common sense is seen as a "sixth sense" that, unlike our five bodily senses, is not private and incommunicable but rather is public and shared (*LM:T,* 50). For Kant (Arendt does not make clear her position), failure to participate in common sense, to have only *sensus privatus,* is insanity. Arendt, *LK,* 64.

39. *LM:T,* 69, 192–93, 215; *LK,* 4. See also Young-Bruehl, *Mind and the Body Politic,* 92–94.

40. Hannah Arendt, "The Crisis in Culture," in *Between Past and Future,* 220. Hereafter cited CC. Many commentaries on Arendt's conception of judgment have struggled with her unpolished lecture notes (published posthumously as *Lectures on Kant's Political Philosophy*), overlooking the lucid section of this earlier essay, in which Arendt has already concluded that the *Critique of Judgment* "contains perhaps the greatest and most original aspect of Kant's political philosophy" (219).

41. See Disch, *Hannah Arendt and the Limits of Philosophy,* 150–51.

42. Tracy Strong emphasized to me that Arendt believed that private sensations are not subject to argument because they are not susceptible to representation *(De gustibus non est disputandum).* Yet to neglect private sensations because they do not allow representation is to assume the priority of representation over intervention. For an illuminating dissent from this assumption, see Ian Hacking, *Representing and Intervening* (Cambridge: Cambridge University Press, 1983). In chapter 4 I develop a conception of reflection involving intervention into seemingly unrepresentable dimensions of the self.

43. The respective failures of Kant and Arendt to make such work on the self an aspect of reflection are discussed in William E. Connolly, "A Critique of Pure Politics," in *Why I Am Not a Secularist* (Minneapolis: University of Minnesota Press, 1999), 163–87.

2

A DIRECTION IN BEING

EMBODIMENT AND TELEOLOGY IN CHARLES TAYLOR

The human subject . . . is an embodied subject. . . . [T]his is easy to say, and hard to understand exactly. . . . [A] great deal of modern thought is based on either ignoring [this], or trying by various means to circumvent [it]. That is why what is involved must be spelled out.

—Charles Taylor

As I argued in the preceding chapter, too little attention is given to a crucial dimension of thought and action, and of ethics and politics: human embodiment. Embodiment requires attention for a number of reasons. Our embodied selves—characterized as we are by varying and fluctuating capacities, needs, feelings, desires, inclinations, and aversions—are not fully understood by us yet are involved in our thinking and acting. Seldom are our embodied selves congruent with the moral and political order in which we find ourselves, yet we strive for such congruence. There are limits to this, since at least some embodied selves will remain incongruent with a given order, while every order—necessarily, it seems—strives for some degree of congruence and must concern itself with subjects whose embodiment deviates from its ideals, expectations, and requirements.

Individuals have little choice, then, but to attend to the relation of their embodied selves to the moral and political order to which they are subject and to respond to the incongruence. They may respond by altering their bodies to better align them with the order in which they live (e.g., diets, cosmetic surgery, psychiatric medication, "stress management") or by challenging the order to better align it with their bodies (e.g., the Americans with Disabilities Act, feminist challenges to aesthetics of beauty, employee demands that the workplace be redesigned). Deciding how to respond is complicated, as our bodies are the way they are owing in part to the order in which we live, and our evaluation of this order is influenced importantly by our bodies.

As these formulations convey, reflection on embodiment is inescapably circular, often dizzyingly complex, and never complete. Consequently, attention to embodiment might be *ongoing* (which is not to say *all-consuming*), not promising a final solution but still of value, and its neglect costly. We might attend to our embodiment, seeking practices of reflection that give prominence to it and ethical sensibilities and social arrangements that better express it. We might acknowledge that governing embodied subjects involves discipline and normalization yet seek ways in which this can be more thoughtful, careful, and acceptable.

Charles Taylor would resist some of these statements. Emphasis on embodiment pervades his thought, and he views the body far more affirmatively than does Arendt. His resistance stems largely from his conception of the body as teleological, as having an intrinsic "bent" toward certain paths of development. This allows him to hope for morality and communities that are experienced more as attunement than as imposition and for forms of inclusion that do not entail exclusion. As does Arendt, Taylor covers a tremendous range of philosophical and political topics, and to tease out his assumptions regarding the body, one must work through his interconnected conceptions of language, selfhood, agency, reflection, community, ethics, and politics. Since the body figures crucially in these conceptions, challenges to Taylor's assumptions regarding the body ramify and reverberate throughout his other conceptions, and alternative assumptions require us to revise these conceptions.[1]

Using the body as a point of reference, I explore Taylor's formulations regarding language and feeling, embodiment and rationality, freedom and morality, understanding and action, and reflection and criticism. My exploration ranges across Taylor's writings, as he seldom expresses a position once and for all but rather returns to certain themes again and again, as he attempts to "articulate" them and to accentuate in one place dimensions that remained in the background in his other discussions. Although there are exceptions and countertendencies in his thinking, my exposition and criticism center on his dominant tendencies. To employ a term Taylor makes much use of, my concern is the direction in which his position *slopes*.[2]

LANGUAGE AND FEELING

Taylor argues that "our interpretation of ourselves and our experience is constitutive of what we are."[3] Human subjectivity and emotion are constituted in part by a particular language and consequently are best characterized through this language. Although inextricable, there is no simple order or relation between language and understanding on the one hand and experience and objects on the other. With regard to the emotions, language and understanding are inspired by various emotions, in turn allowing their clarification and crystallization, their description and redescription, facilitating their evaluation, and helping into being new emotions.

Language allows us to characterize and clarify what are, prior to their characterization, simpler, amorphous, and clouded feelings, and these new, clearer feelings inspire new expressions in language (SIA, 56). Feelings are transformed by language and understanding, in turn making possible new, often more powerful, refined, and lucid feelings.[4] Humans, as language-using, self-interpreting animals, are capable of new, linguistically mediated feelings, reflecting richer experiences and a more complex sense of the world than could be attained without language (SIA, 56).

We are constituted in part, but *only in part*, by our self-understandings and our vocabularies of emotion and import.[5] It is the profound but limited role of language—constitutive of selfhood and society but not wholly comprising them, indispensable but never adequate for understanding them—that makes this matter so difficult to grasp. Emotional life includes phenomena that are enabled and crucially shaped by a vocabulary of import, but that involve desires, feelings, inclinations, wants, fears, and the like that are in some respects independent of the vocabulary of import, and that often precede or outlive it.

We can imagine, for example, a child with certain desires growing up in a society that has no place for her desires. This requires her, in some manner, to conceal, ignore, subordinate, or modify her desires or to contest the inhospitable vocabulary of import in which she finds herself. And we can imagine an adult leaving a religious order that has a certain vocabulary of import and returning to society and assuming another vocabulary, yet still harboring lingering feelings (residual inhibitions, perhaps, that were consolidated by the religious order's enforced morality, codes of conduct, and routines of living) that have no place in his new vocabulary of import. Nevertheless, his earlier feelings may persist. In both examples, we cannot understand the individual apart from her or his vocabulary of import, but neither can we adequately understand her or him if we attend exclusively to their respective vocabularies.[6]

We cannot, then, neatly separate the linguistic and nonlinguistic, or that resulting from our language of import and that which is independent of it. Rather, we reside in a coil of subjectivity in which "import and goal, the language of feelings and consummations desired, form a skein of mutual referrals, from which there is no escape into objectified nature" (SIA, 57). Sentiments underlie morals, feelings enter evaluation, intuitive grasps sustain explanations—not in temporal or logical priority, but in mutual constitution and sustenance. Reflection and argument involve articulation of the inarticulate and rely on the intuitive and the implicit. The intuitive and implicit often exceed articulations, seeping into and sustaining them, though not fully amenable to them.[7]

The process of articulation is exploratory and ongoing, as the inarticulate—feelings, moods, inclinations, intuitions, implicit understandings—gives rise to and challenges our articulations. We sense the adequacy and clarity of present articulations and are inspired to advance them further. Through this process, we modify and cultivate sentiments and develop new ones, in turn arriving at fresh articulations and giving rise to new questions. Our articulations "go deeper" into our feelings, identifying them and making them more explicit and expressing the sense of import underlying and shaping them. A language of import allows "fuller and richer" articulation of our feelings (SIA, 56). Articulations bring to explicit awareness what we formerly had only an implicit sense of, lifting it above the surface, to fuller and clearer consciousness (TM, 256–57). Seldom do we accomplish this in a simple or decisive step. Rather, we struggle to find an adequate articulation and often are not satisfied with the one we have found. And following articulation, that which was not adequately captured in the articulation remains to challenge it, prompting us to strive for further, more satisfying articulation (SIA, 75).[8]

Self-interpretation involves discernment and evaluation. We discern and evaluate our emotions and desires through the prism of our vocabulary of import and notions of the good life, which are themselves kept alive by our emotions and desires (SIA, 65). "Strong evaluations" embody our most general, fundamental notions of import and the good life, allowing us to assess feelings, desires, and aspirations, while stemming in part from them (SIA, 65–67). Strong evaluations are not appendages to the self but partly constitute it, as selfhood and agency are not possible without such fundamental, constitutive notions of import and value.[9] Strong evaluations underlie our language and culture, making possible "characteristically human concerns" (TM, 260). For example, humans, along with (we may conjecture) some animals, can experience the emotion of anger. But only the mature human, given notions of justice and desert, can experience indignation. Indignation involves feelings and bodily activity similar to those involved in anger, but it is also constituted by certain notions and values in a way that the simpler emotion of anger is not.

Characteristically human emotions, such as indignation, then, cannot exist independently of a language of import, but neither are they wholly contained in that language, independent of feelings and bodily activity. Indeed, strong evaluations, our most basic senses of import and value, become *corporealized;* they come to reside not merely in intellect, narrowly conceived, but also in our bodies. Our most basic sense of import and value is often powerfully felt, so much so that it feels like instinct, or in some way natural. Our modern aversion to the undeserved suffering of others, for example, seems little different from our aversion to nauseating substances (SS, 4–5). In this respect, our sense of import and value, though to some extent articulable, resides in part in "'gut' feelings" (SS, 7).[10]

As reflective subjects, in giving sustained attention to the relation between our strong evaluations, inchoate sentiments, and deepest feelings, we draw "a moral map of ourselves" and in doing so clarify and further shape our experience (SIA, 67). Maps of ourselves chart, in a rough manner, current and long-standing conditions in the landscape of our feelings, moods, desires, inclinations, and needs. Our map is never entirely clear or complete, and it requires continual updating and revision as conditions change and contours of the terrain shift. In sketching this topography, we identify the values, sentiments, and feelings that constitute us and, in identifying them, begin to reconstitute ourselves, as we evaluate, accentuate, and modify certain values, sentiments and feelings.[11] In this process we make judgments, often murkily, as our relative attachments to goods and the varying intensities of our feelings lead us to choices and priorities.[12]

Reflective awareness and heightened consciousness involve formulating such orders of importance and significance, discerning tendencies and priorities, and achieving a more articulate view of ourselves.[13] Ethical reflection consists in part in assessing these competing demands on ourselves, recognizing some as higher, and distinguishing conflicting desires and goals (CP, 102). Importantly, although he insists on the imbrication of language and emotion, Taylor resists providing a model of strict causation or precisely locating insight into our emotions.[14] To do so would be to account for emotion-insights as one accounts for external objects, rather than as that which partly constitute the subject studying them and which are changed as soon as they are studied. Dispassionate observation and refined representation are not available, nor would they be sufficient. The situation, rather, is one of proximity and subtlety, in which the subject is inherently implicated in that being accounted for.

This belief is central to Taylor's thought and underlies his categorical, Diltheyan distinction between the study of humans and the study of nature. The two domains are presented as ontologically distinct, hence requiring distinct epistemologies (respectively, interpretation, and observation).[15] An important consequence of this belief is that, since human life is crucially constituted by language, accounts of a particular form of life must employ the particular language constituting it. Moreover, subject-centered accounts are given priority, and accounts that invalidate them—that is, accounts that displace or discredit the language constituting the subject—seem to be ruled out. This is based "simply on the impossibility of believing that we have been talking nonsense all these millennia."[16] I return to this claim below.

For Taylor, the worst thing we can do when dealing with the presence of feelings in thought is to respond with denial or dismay, attempting to ignore or expunge them—something he alleges many moderns have done, and which Arendt leans toward doing. Nor should we, as Taylor contends utilitarians have done, reduce thinking to a simple inventory of brute feelings and wants. Rather, we must acknowledge feelings and moods as elements *within* thought itself and make attention to them part of thinking (SIA, 59–62). For example, we have all met individuals (particularly those who confidently present themselves as rationalists) who seem oblivious to subtleties of feeling and mood. We often view such individuals as, in important respects, insensitive and unreflective, and we worry that their treatment of sensitive matters would be so unfeeling that we are reluctant to entrust them with such matters.

Taylor's position regarding the presence of feeling in thought, then, is interestingly different from that of both rationalists such as Kant and non-rationalists such as Nietzsche. For Kant, reason is a faculty that is the same across individuals, leading individuals to arrive, if only practical reason is relied on, at the same morality. If individual feeling—bodily impulses and contrary inclinations—enter thinking, then individuals will not necessarily arrive at the same morality. Taylor rejects (or, at least, radically revises) Kantian rationalism, seeing feeling as importantly and deservedly entering thinking. However, in order to give feeling an important role in thinking and to retain his commitments—not Kant's vision of universal moral agreement, but an ideal of unity—Taylor must conceive of individual bodily constitution and feeling as not radically variant. If individual constitution and feeling are not radically variant, then neither will be the feeling-imbued morality arrived at by individuals. If, against Kant, we agree with Taylor on the insufficiency of rationality for arriving at morality but, against Taylor, emphasize the diversity of individual constitution and feeling, then we are led to emphasize the diversity of individual and cultural moralities. This is essentially Nietzsche's position.

EMBODIMENT AND RATIONALITY

In *Hegel and Modern Society* Taylor presents a detailed exposition of Hegel's conception of the embodied subject.[17] Although he does not state his ultimate agreement or disagreement, Taylor acknowledges his indebtedness to Hegel. For this reason, examining his exposition of Hegel helps to understand Taylor's positions regarding embodiment and rationality.

For Hegel, in Taylor's exposition, the opposition between freedom and nature, the individual and society, subject and world, and man and God can be overcome. Unity can be achieved between free rational consciousness on the one hand and nature, society, God, and fate on the other (*HMS,* 14). Philosophy facilitates reconciliation, bringing this unity to consciousness and contributing to its realization. Taylor explains our predicament:

> Man only attains his self-conscious, rational autonomy in separating off from nature, society, God and fate; he only wins through to inner freedom by disciplining natural impulse in himself, breaking from the unthinking bent of social custom, challenging the authority of God and sovereign, refusing to accept the decrees of fate. And Hegel sees this very clearly, which is why he repudiates any attempt simply to undo the opposition and return to primitive unity. (*HMS,* 15)

Unity—within ourselves, with others, and with the world—is shattered as we mature toward freedom and rational consciousness. Once such unity is lost, it takes a long time and tremendous effort to get it back.

This is nevertheless what Hegel seeks. Hegel's conception of the modern subject is said to combine, among many influences, Herder's expressivism and Aristotle's realization of purpose. In Hegel's conception, the subject clarifies what it is through expression and in doing so progresses toward self-realization (*HMS,* 16). Taylor presents this position as "radically anti-dualist," in that it conceives of consciousness as inseparable from the body. Dualism, in which the body is reduced to a mere object, exemplified by Descartes's separation of mind from body, is incompatible with the Aristotelian conception of life. In the latter, form, approximated through purposiveness and intelligence, is inseparable from its material embodiment (*HMS,* 17). In this conception, even abstract and formal thought is embodied, in that its medium of expression—language—is bound up with ways of being. Thus, the content of thought is always "couched in an external medium" (*HMS*, 18). Also, crucially, rationality is not a mere appendage to humans, since "reflective consciousness leaves nothing unaltered" (*HMS*, 19). Our feelings and desires, bearing and posture are changed by it.[18]

Moreover, influenced in part by Kant, Hegel views consciousness not only as permeating life but also as *negating* life. Consciousness does so because humans have attempted to separate and insulate rational thought from desire and unconscious inclination. (Kant wants this separation, whereas Hegel and Taylor want to overcome it.) "Man is thus inescapably at odds with himself," as thinking is part of living yet turns against life, leading to internal discord in the subject (*HMS*, 20). Consequently, advances in consciousness require strenuous effort, as we struggle with internal division. In doing so, we transform impulse and give shape to our lives, molding ourselves to fit a culture of rationality and freedom (*HMS*, 21). In this sense, we are both inseparable from, and opposed to, our embodiment.

And yet, for Hegel (Taylor himself is less optimistic) this opposition can be reconciled and a higher unity achieved:

> Raw nature, the life of impulse, is made over, cultivated, so as to reflect the higher aspirations of man, to be an expression of reason. And reason, on the other side, ceases to identify itself narrowly with a supposedly higher self fighting to hold nature at bay. (*HMS*, 22)

As arduous as it may be, ultimately the two can be brought into (or, for Taylor, toward) alignment. Hegel thus restored the sense of "*continuity within ourselves* between vital and mental functions, life and consciousness" (*HMS*, 19, emphasis mine). Taylor never stops pursuing such reconciliation and unity, though he laments that they may never be achieved. Indeed, he relies on their possibility, or at least on their *ideal*, when framing other matters. Inspired by Hegel, Taylor upholds an ideal in which political intersubjectivity is aligned with the embodied self; that is, in which the latter is less in conflict with, than encompassed by, the former.

Having introduced Taylor's treatment of embodiment by summarizing his reading of Hegel, we can elaborate Taylor's principal claim—that we are *essentially, inescapably* embodied—considering the nature and implications of the claim. "The human subject," begins Taylor in his essay "Embodied Agency," is "an embodied subject."[19] This claim, he explains, is easy to say but difficult to understand. And although the claim seems to be undeniable, it is not clear how we might demonstrate it or what status such a demonstration would assume.[20] Nevertheless, although nobody would deny that humans are embodied, not everybody mentions human embodiment.[21]

Taylor wishes to argue not simply, as a point of fact, that the human subject is embodied or that being a subject requires certain bodily equipment, but the stronger, deeper thesis that our "*manner of being* as subjects is in essential respects that of embodied agents" (EA, 3, emphasis mine). This needs to be shown, he believes—not demonstrated but rather articulated, articulated so as to be undeniable. Relying on Merleau-Ponty, Taylor argues that perception is basic to us as subjects. It is so because we are always perceiving; we can never entirely shut the world out but are variously open to it at different moments, owing in part to the extent to which our disposition is one of receptiveness. Perception also orients us to the world, providing the foundational background that allows us to understand more abstract or distant matters.

Perception is not that of a detached, disengaged subject but that of an agent, influenced by, engaged in, and acting in the world she is perceiving (EA, 4). "Our perceptual field has an orientational structure" that situates us in the world and allows us to maintain a coherent stance toward it, giving us a secure grasp and allowing comprehension and effective action (EA, 4, 6). Taylor wishes to argue, then, not merely that perception occurs in a particular body but, more fundamentally, that our perception is *constituted* by our embodiment, that our field of perception is structured by our embodied relation to the world as subjects and agents (EA, 8).[22]

Not to have such a stable orientational structure, Taylor explains, is to descend into the nightmare of disorientation and dislocation, of losing one's grip: "[I]n those rare moments when I lose track of my bodily action; those terrible moments of confusion, when I don't know any more what I'm doing or where my limbs are, I have also lost track of my world" (EA, 20 n. 2). Such terrible moments are palpable in Cuban novelist Alejo Carpentier's book *The Chase*,[23] in which a nameless protagonist being pursued by government assassins is, in his final hours, overwhelmed by hunger, exhaustion, and confusion; in which his hallucinatory, stumbling journey through darkness ends, suggestively, as he seeks refuge in a concert performance of a beautiful, familiar symphony, his world having become a terrifying, bewildering cacophony.

Alternatively, *productive* disorientation is portrayed by Nietzsche in a passage in which "the madman," upon seeing that God is dead, asks "Whither are we moving? Away from all suns? Are we not plunging continually? Backward, sideward, forward, in all directions? Is there still any up or down? . . . Has it not become colder? Is not night continually closing in on us? Do we not need light lanterns in the morning?"[24] The emphasis here is on the way in which conceptual disorientation leads to perceptual disorientation. Unlike Taylor, Nietzsche values—on occasion, within limits—disorientation. It is valued because it can serve to unsettle one's stable orientational structure—reconfiguring Taylor's "zones of accessibility and inaccessibility" (EA, 5)—making possible experiences previously unavailable and hence enabling deeper, more radical reflection.

These views of Taylor's are not exactly, he notes, part of an *ontological* thesis. That is, his argument is that "we are inescapably to ourselves embodied subjects" (EA, 14). We must be so, since to be a subject, to comprehend our world and to act effectively in it, requires an orientational structure that is constituted by our embodied location and perception. Typically, it is argued (as Taylor himself has argued) that this proves an ontological thesis: that what we inescapably *are to ourselves* is what we *truly are*. In this view, attempts to understand humans, such as the many social scientific attempts that are not rooted in what we are to ourselves, always miss the mark. However, crucially, in "Embodied Agency" Taylor concedes that this stronger ontological conclusion does not necessarily follow. Instead,

> the possibility remains open that what we are to ourselves may be in important ways misleading; that a deeper level explanation of the functioning of human beings might be based on quite other principles. [I]n this case, our sense of self would be an obstacle to our deeper understanding of how we function. (EA, 14)

This is a significant concession. As we shall explore in the final section of this chapter, it allows the possibility that our understandings of ourselves and of our society, even though in part constituting ourselves and our society, may be challenged as inadequate or misleading. Previously, Taylor has emphasized the possibility of distorted understandings, maintaining that such distortions can be removed by articulating our true, deeper, constitutive understandings. Yet here he allows the possibility of newer understandings not so based and of *multiple, competing understandings, none of which can claim the deepest hold.* Instead, all understandings may be incomplete—they may block out experiences made possible by other understandings and may stifle dimensions of life enabled by others. Consequently, we might strive to *live between* two or more understandings of ourselves, variously inhabiting them and playing them off one another (what Hampshire terms "seeing double"). In this view, *every* self-understanding is, in part, a misunderstanding and (often arbitrary) limitation. Taylor does not return to this point, yet we shall do so.[25]

Taylor proceeds in this essay to discuss how embodiment "sets the framework" for identity, how we come to see that we are "essentially this body" (EA, 16). In the standard materialist conception (more sophisticated versions of which appear in Nietzsche and Hampshire), we are identical to our bodies, and the body is nothing more than "a machine whose limits and basic thrust has to be accepted" (EA, 16). Alternatively, in Taylor's conception of embodiment, with its notions of telos and purpose, the

> body is already a direction of life, partly sketched, and the locus of the as yet undetermined. This is the direction of life which I have to take up as I define it. In this way, my embodied being sets the framework for any identity I may be able to define as a person. (EA, 16)

Taylor distinguishes this position, rightly, from that of reductionist materialists, who he contends view the body crudely as a simple object, and from that of those who present identity as unconstrained by embodiment. Taylor does not, however, fully distinguish his teleological, purposive conception of embodiment from conceptions such as Nietzsche's, and to the extent that he does, he dismisses them. Such conceptions also see the subject as essentially embodied and concur that the subject's body sets the framework for identity, but they see bodily development and expression as more ambiguous than does Taylor, as involving not only attunement but also dissonance. That is, materialists such as Nietzsche and Hampshire emphasize that embodiment entails not a single direction of life but rather multiple, contradictory directions, not all of which can be expressed in a particular identity. Multiple, contradictory directions of life are found not only among individuals but also, more challengingly, *within* individuals.

Other important elements in Taylor's treatment of embodiment include the order of desires; the manner in which language, understanding, and culture are encoded in the body; and the assumption that humans have a bent toward certain paths of moral development. These elements are discussed in the remaining sections of this chapter.

FREEDOM AND MORALITY

Most well known in Taylor's treatment of freedom is his defense of positive freedom (an "exercise-concept") alongside negative freedom (a mere "opportunity-concept").[26] Embedded in his analysis, and in his related discussions of agency and individuality, is a treatment of the body that is illuminating in many respects and limiting in others. Central to Taylor's treatment, and most significant for our inquiry, are his conception of an order of desires and his assumption of human purpose, which are seen as requirements for evaluation, identity, freedom, and agency. As we shall see, the hermeneutic circularity of language and feeling emphasized earlier, in which there is no possibility of getting beneath the "skein of mutual referrals" in order to uncover an unshifting bedrock of the self, stands in tension with his belief that we can do so, that we can identify essential desires and purposes beneath inessential desires and pursuits. Taylor's other theoretical commitments make it difficult to uphold this belief, but his political commitments encourage him to uphold it.

Conceptions of negative freedom are said to make no distinction, at base, between types of desire. Instead, desires have the character of being "raw" or "brute," as they are independent of evaluation (NL, 223). Evaluation consists, in this conception, of weighing, measuring, or calculating the strength and balance of our desires. Against this, Taylor maintains that the richer conception of positive freedom denies that there can be raw or brute desires, wholly independent of evaluation; it denies that evaluation consists of the mere weighing of desires; and it denies that freedom consists merely of satisfying undistinguished, qualitatively equivalent desires.

Animals, we assume, have a single order of desires (e.g., to eat at one moment, to sleep at the next). Their desires vary in frequency and intensity and at times conflict, but they exist on the same plane. Humans—and this is conceived as *distinguishing* humans—have a higher, or second, order of desires, allowing us to distinguish some desires as more desirable (WHA, 15). We often identify what is felt to be a strong, immediate desire, such as to take a nap, as not *really* desirable, as it conflicts with a higher, second order desire to, for example, complete a lengthy book chapter.

Taylor's distinction is useful. We should not dispense with it, nor should we adopt a crude utilitarianism in which evaluation and choice consist of the mere weighing of desires. Rather, my concern is the emphasis in Taylor's position, as it leans strongly toward ascribing so much importance to second-order desires as to neglect or subordinate first-order desires. Taylor assures us, without explanation, that he is not committing himself to the notion of a higher and a lower self (NL, 216), but his position slopes toward this. We can agree with Taylor that second-order desires *distinguish* humans without saying that they are always most important to humans, or that evaluation and identity *principally* involve second-order desires (just as we could say earlier that humans are *language* animals without ascribing singular importance to language).

The issue of sexual choice and identity is illuminating, in part because sexual desire is often presented as the paradigm of lower desires and because most moralities include some notion of higher values that restrict sexual desire and activity. We can imagine an individual conforming to Taylor's portrait of reflection and evaluation, in which the individual realizes that satisfying his desire for sexual variety (which requires him to devote much time to seeking new sexual partners) prevents him from satisfying what he comes to identify as his "higher" desire to settle down with one partner and experience the security and satisfaction of companionship. When making this choice he cannot be guided simply by the strength of his desire for sexual variety, since he himself wishes that this desire were not so strong. In this scenario, his choice to settle for monogamy involves second-order desires.

But we can also imagine the case of an individual who, despite family and religious expectations to pursue marriage and motherhood, powerfully feels her "lower" sexual desire for women. Her lower desire may clamor for satisfaction and be fundamental to her needs and constitution, even though she has a second-order desire to pursue marriage and motherhood so as not to upset her family or lapse in her religious commitments. In Taylor's model of reflection she is not encouraged to allow her first-order desire to challenge or trump her second-order desire. For Taylor, reflection and evaluation involve getting beyond our first-order desires to identify our second-order desires but seldom involve privileging the first over the second or allowing the first to loosen the second. Taylor might reformulate this example to fit his model, saying that the woman, if she chose to express her lesbianism, was identifying her highest- (or third- or fourth-) order desire (viz., to live authentically).

Such a reformulation is not unconvincing, but it can be contrasted with other approaches. Another approach would differ in two respects. First, emphasis would be placed not only on identifying our highest values (Taylor's second-order desires) but also on identifying desires and instincts (Taylor's first-order desires) that may be neglected, suppressed, or devalued by our highest values. This approach would encourage the woman in the above scenario to allow her first-order desires to *unsettle* her second-order desires. This does not necessarily invert Taylor's hierarchy, giving priority to first-order desires, but rather sees reflection and evaluation as a set of *less charted encounters* between first- and second-order desires, in which neither has inherent priority. Instead of a dialectical relation between two orders of desire, this approach portrays a *layered corporeality* involving multiple orders of desire.[27]

Second, to modify the example slightly, let us say that the woman's deepest commitments are to her family and her religion and that her desire for women is matched by her desire for men. In Taylor's conception, given her other commitments and desires, she would come to see her desire for women as not "really" part of herself. Her lesbian tendencies would be seen

55

as an inessential part of herself, since they threaten to undermine that which she most values. For Taylor, identity does not require the sacrifice of desires seen as essential or truly important but rather involves coming to see desires that cannot be contained in our identity as "not ours," and hence inessential or unimportant (NL, 225).

Alternatively, the woman would not necessarily dissociate herself from her desire for women or deny that this desire is an essential part of herself, even if she chose not to pursue it or to subordinate it to other values and to cultivate other aspects of herself. She might not seek to eliminate all such tensions, contradictions, and forfeitures in the organization of herself. Rather, she might harbor such tensions, contradictions, and forfeitures, realizing that no identity or lifestyle can accommodate all of her needs and desires or allow all admirable possibilities of being. Taylor rejects such a position, which he attributes to Nietzsche, as it sees morality as always "crushing much that is elemental and instinctive in us" and hence sees authenticity as in tension with any single morality or identity.[28] The alternative position is more demanding, but it promises a fuller, more nuanced conception of authenticity than Taylor provides.

UNDERSTANDING AND ACTION

In "To Follow a Rule," while developing an original interpretation of Wittgenstein's much discussed treatment of this topic, Taylor formulates the dependence of thought and community on embodiment, assuming the *stabilizing* effect of the body.[29] His formulations thus provide an alternative to Nietzsche's assumption of the destablizing effect of the body. In developing his interpretation, Taylor lays out his view of the connections between embodied understanding, social practices, common meaning, and public space.

Taylor's query begins with the following scenario found in Wittgenstein's *Philosophical Investigations*. Consider a common cultural symbol, such as a road sign with an arrow on it. None of us is confused, not even for a moment, when encountering the symbol. Yet if we were to pause, we would realize, at some point, that there are many, indeed an infinitely large number of, possible interpretations of the symbol. We could appeal to additional rules to justify our interpretation, but each rule would itself spawn further confusion and doubt. Every justification for our interpretation would require further justification. Wittgenstein's point is that the subject *could not* be aware of all the issues related to the correct interpretation of the symbol or rule and of all the alternative interpretations, as this exceeds the capacity of any mind (TFR, 165).

However, Taylor believes that our "intellectualist philosophical culture" assumes that somewhere *in our mind* is a whole set of premises underlying our interpretation (TFR, 165). There are at least two alternatives to this intellectualist position, in which interpretation and action require an underlying set of premises. Both alternatives presume, instead, that every interpretation of a rule involves a "phronetic gap," a gap that no number of additional rules will close. The first alternative, offered by Saul Kripke, holds that rule-following is often little more than brute reaction; sufficient reasons cannot be given for our particular interpretation.[30] The second alternative, offered by Taylor, presumes an entire shared background giving sense to rules and stability to conventions, resting on common, inchoate, embodied understanding. Such understanding can be partially articulated and formulated to meet particular queries and challenges, but for the most part it remains inarticulate and unformulated (TFR, 168). That is, *at any moment* more remains in our background understanding than in the foreground, but that which is in the foreground, and thus in focus, articulable, and allowing scrutiny, shifts.[31]

Taylor wishes to emphasize, first, that the presence of a shared background for thought and meaningful action is crucial and, second, that this background is both social and embodied. Doing so allows him to present conceptions of selfhood and thinking as embodied and socially embedded, in contrast to the "modern" view of them as disembodied and disengaged. And it allows him to see the body and society as less in tension than in cooperation. In the dominant, modern view the "disengaged first-person-singular self" (said to originate in Descartes and seen again in Locke and Kant), "what 'I' am . . . the inner space itself, is definable independently of body or other. It is a center of monological consciousness" (TFR, 169). For Taylor there cannot be disembodied, monological consciousness, since consciousness rests on background understandings, which are embodied and socially embedded.

The underlying, embodied background to thought, then, precedes thinking. The background is, for the most part, inherited socially and sets limits to our experience and thinking. Taylor appreciates the ways in which altering this background alters our experience and thinking and in doing so makes possible new modes of being. And he sometimes appreciates the extent to which new, uncanny experiences may disturb our settled background understanding, requiring significant, sometimes radical, revision of it. However, Taylor's repeated emphases on the familiarity, coherence, and stability of background understanding lead him to value far too little the disturbance and destabilization of settled, shared background understandings. In places these tendencies are stronger than mere emphases, as when Taylor presents the "a priori," "apodictic," "unchallengeable," "indispensable" claim "that experience must be coherent to be experience."[32]

Combining Wittgenstein with Heidegger and Merleau-Ponty, Taylor urges that we "see the agent not primarily as the locus of representations, but as engaged in practices, as a being who acts in and on the world" (TFR, 170). Understanding resides in practices and thus is implicit in our activity. Intelligent action and bodily performance "flow from an understanding that is largely inarticulate" (TFR, 170). An unformulated grasp of the world is present in most situations, and mental representations occur *within* it. Taylor's formulation

> puts the role of the body in a new light. Our body is not just the executant of the goals we frame, nor just the locus of causal factors shaping our representations. *Our understanding is itself embodied.* That is, our bodily know-how, and the way we act and move, can encode components of our understanding of self and world. (TFR, 170, emphasis mine).

Along with our grasp of a situation, the sense and image we have of ourselves are in large part embodied. Our attitudes toward others and how we project ourselves in social situations and public space are encoded in our posture, movement, and body language (TFR, 171). We see this, for example, when an individual comes across as calm, confident, aggressive, timid, or nervous. Our body language manifests many of our values and understandings, which are encoded in the body and composed of certain feelings, desires, postures, movements, reactions, and the like.[33]

So even though we often lack the language to articulate our embodied understandings, these understandings are crucially present, as they underlie, usually securely, our thinking, sense of self, and social relations. Indeed, the following of rules, indispensable for any social order, requires that an inarticulate sense of appropriate action be encoded in the body (TFR, 180). Drawing on Pierre Bourdieu, Taylor introduces the notion of "'habitus'"—"'a system of durable and transposable dispositions'" encoded in the body (TFR, 178). By inculcating the appropriate habitus, children are inducted into a culture and thus internalize a set of meanings and values, which they then help to sustain. In this respect, Taylor explains, rules exist in our lives as "'values made flesh'" (TFR, 179). Some rules are expressly formulated and reside in our explicit awareness, but most rules (if they can be called that) are not so formulated and remain beneath such awareness. Even expressly formulated rules require for their activation an underpinning of unformulated, embodied understanding. The effort often required to make values flesh—an effort involving, in Nietzsche's judgment, a certain amount of violence—is something Taylor never attends to.

The connection between embodiment and society is illuminated further if we consider the pervasiveness of common action; that is, action consisting not simply of the coordination of individuals but requiring an "integrated, nonindividual agent," such as a couple dancing (TFR, 172). A great deal of human activity involves common action, in which the individual constitutes herself as an integral part of a "'we.'" In such activity, we define ourselves partly with reference to our place within dialogical, common action, as we contribute to, and are in part constituted by, such action. And "language itself serves to set up spaces of common action, on a number of levels, intimate and public" (TFR, 173).

Taylor's distinction between individual and common action, in which the latter is irreducible to the former, is similar to Arendt's conception of action. Yet Arendt speaks little of *individual* action; action for her is primarily a collective phenomenon in which individuals achieve concert. And Arendt views laboring together, with its coordinated rhythms and motions, as fundamentally deindividualizing, as it reduces us to our bodily sameness. At a number of points Taylor upholds Arendt's conception of action. Importantly, he invokes Arendt when challenging Foucault's insistence that common action will always be felt—in certain respects, for certain individuals—as imposition and hence that common action not only empowers but also disempowers.[34]

Nevertheless, Taylor's emphasis on the embodied quality of the public realm and common action is importantly contrary to other conceptions. As Michael Warner argues, the public realm, since its modern inception and as conceived by contemporaries such as Habermas, has typically relied on the fiction of disembodiment—as arguments are to be abstracted from the particular embodied location of those presenting them. When discourse is governed by an ideal of disembodiment, it is difficult to challenge implicit, disadvantageous assumptions about individual embodiment. This is not an accident, as the bourgeois public realm, with its exclusions and silences regarding race, gender, sexuality and class, required that discussion of embodiment remain difficult, thereby preventing politics from "getting personal."[35]

A fascinating discussion of common action, in which rhythmic exercise and ritual are relied on to inculcate solidarity and constitute community, is military historian William H. McNeill's *Keeping Together in Time: Dance and Drill in Human History.*[36] McNeill focuses on less innocuous forms of common action than does Taylor, ones more fundamental to social and political order, namely, preparation for war. McNeill's analysis is consistent with Taylor's, as he concludes that obedience among troops—which culminates, ideally, not in mere willingness to attack a designated enemy but eagerness for such opportunities—does not depend simply on instructions for combat, nor on a set of rules or rewards, nor on a particular ideology. Rather, effective military preparation requires rituals and exercises—bodily activities that arouse the troops, cultivating certain feelings and leading to excitement, euphoria, and "'muscular bonding'" (vi). When successful, as it often is, the outcome is for troops to experience "'[b]oundary loss'" and "'feeling they are one'" (8). In short, they are constituted as Taylor's integrated nonindividual agent. As one soldier explains: many veterans feel that "the experience of communal effort in battle . . . has been the high point of their lives. . . . Their 'I' passes insensibly into a 'we,' 'my' becomes 'our,' and individual fate loses its central importance." McNeill concludes, "Moving our muscles rhythmically and giving voice consolidate group solidarity by altering human feelings" (vii). "We are captives of language for our explanations, and words do not capture the visceral emotions aroused by keeping together in time" (10).[37]

Moreover, an unavoidable consequence of common action and thickening social cohesion, which Taylor seldom attends to, is that "marginalized persons multipl[y]" (57). They must multiply, as common action and general standards make demands that some persons fail to meet. These persons become marginal, as their failures and foot-dragging detract from common action, and they are likely to be resented for this.[38]

Thus, to Taylor's satisfaction, appreciation of the dependence of shared background understandings on individual embodiment allows us to account for the phenomena of regular rule-following and, more generally, common action, given the possibility of utter chaos. Stable understandings and practices require stable bodies. Nonexclusionary common action requires principally similar bodies. For Taylor, it is best to assume that this is what we have.

REFLECTION AND CRITICISM

In Taylor's formulations regarding language and feeling, embodiment and rationality, freedom and morality, and understanding and action, we see how, though he strays from it at points, he repeatedly returns to a teleology, to an assumption of human purpose and ends, and to an ideal of social unity. Though it is never fully achieved, we are to work toward attunement between our embodied selves and our individual and collective aspirations. Taylor's teleology sustains his hope for settled community, social inclusion, defensible evaluation, and discernible progress. Yet when assumptions of teleology are questioned, as in the next chapter, Taylor's hopes are significantly challenged. Instead, we are led to emphasize the precariousness of community, the limits to social inclusion, the insecure bases for evaluation, and the ambiguity of progress.[39]

Central to Taylor's conceptions of reflection and criticism, and to his disagreement with Nietzsche and Foucault, is his conviction that, in the messy imbrication of language and feeling, although the former does not relate to the latter in terms of verifiable representation, we are able, nevertheless, to speak of the *superiority* of articulations. That is, we can judge some articulations to be superior to others, to be more true to ourselves, and less distortive. This allows us to judge the values and practices—the form of life—that embody these articulations as more true to ourselves. We are thus able to adjudicate forms of life, to identify some as superior, as representing progress or an advance, in that they fit us better and are more true to us. Taylor explains:

> There are more or less adequate, more or less truthful, more self-clairvoyant or self-deluding interpretations. . . . [B]ecause an articulation can be wrong, and yet it shapes what it is wrong about, we sometimes see erroneous articulations as involving a distortion of the reality concerned. (WHA, 38)[40]

As individuals and as a community, we pursue undistorted self-interpretations, continually striving for a form of life that expresses that which we feel to be truly important. I do not reject this ideal, but I uphold it with qualification. Our self-interpretations are better seen as always, in some manner, distorted, and social arrangements as untrue to some aspects of ourselves. This introduces a higher ideal and additional layers to reflection, as ethics now involves attention to the limits and inadequacies of our deepest self-understandings and highest values.

Taylor's position on this matter is elaborated in his assessments of Foucault. Following a patient, probing analysis of Foucault's thought,[41] in a subsequent response to a critic in greater sympathy with Foucault, Taylor concludes that his disagreement with Foucault stems ultimately from his own teleology.[42] Though not one of Platonic Ideas or Hegelian Design, Taylor's teleology presumes that authentic self-understanding "can in a sense be said to follow a *direction in being*" (384–85). A direction in being is essential for Taylor's "'ontology' of the human person," which he believes to be no less defensible than its rivals, including "the Nietzschean notion of truth as imposition" (385).[43] Though acknowledging the incongruity between the embodied self and morality and community, Taylor maintains that self-understanding and social progress consist in achieving greater congruity. Yet he does not attend to the ways in which understanding and progress might involve acknowledging *ineliminable incongruities*. Doing so would enhance the modesty and openness of ethics.

In a later exchange, responding to an essay comparing his thought to that of Foucault,[44] Taylor sharpens the fundamental issue at stake, without clarifying whether *his* commitments have changed (since his earlier insistence that our aspirations must not "run against the grain of [our] basic purposes" [NL, 216]).[45] He concludes that if "one accepts the post-Nietzschean notion that our historic languages have both empowered and victimized, there are roughly three ways one can go" (280). First, one can, following the early Frankfurt school, claim that existing culture goes against "the human grain" and that liberation may rectify this. Second, one can maintain that no human grain can be identified and that we can only choose among incommensurable forms of enablement and victimization. Third, one can deny that there is a human grain and view social forms as incommensurable but still see

> different existential possibilities *within* each package. We can live within a given one, totally absorbed and captured by its language, giving it our uncontested credence and allegiance; or we can live within it with a critical distance, having demystified it precisely thanks to the neo-Nietzschean insight that nothing, and hence not our dominant language, espouses the human grain. This allows [us] . . . to distinguish between packages, to the extent that some inherently give more space for, or are less actively inhospitable to this kind of critical distance. (280)

Such a positive formulation is welcome, but Taylor immediately retreats from it. He understands, as do I, Foucault to have oscillated between the second and third positions, leaning heavily toward the third in his later writings. Though acknowledging the plausibility of each position, Taylor refrains from endorsing any of them, stating only that "irreligious antihumanism [such as Foucault's] can seem so much deeper than all religious humanisms, whereas the question ought to be pressed whether it is not incomparably shallower" (281).[46] We shall ourselves press this question when examining Nietzsche and Hampshire, considering whether irreligious antihumanism is, as Taylor suspects, necessarily shallow and whether there are viable options, individually and socially, for achieving critical distance and more acceptable states of affairs.[47]

Taylor now formulates his conception of strong evaluation in terms of "sources" that orient and sustain thinking and ethical life (*SS,* 91–107). Our attachment to, and dependence on, moral sources is deep:

> Moral sources empower. To come closer to them, to have a clearer view of them, to come to grasp what they involve, is for those who recognize them to be moved to love or respect them, and through this love/respect to be better enabled to live up to them. And articulation can bring them closer. (*SS,* 96)

All of us draw on such moral sources, Taylor contends, and must attempt to articulate what we hold to be good; without doing so, we would not be fully human. Taylor maintains that "the neo-Nietzschean type of theory sees no value in this articulation" (*SS,* 99). This is not entirely correct. Rather, a neo-Nietzschean position, such as the one I have begun to elaborate, values clarifying and coming closer to one's moral sources. But it also values gaining distance from them and identifying the ways in which one's notions of the good limit one's feelings, desires, experiences, and satisfactions; neglect other goods; and close off alternative moral sources.

A neo-Nietzschean position, then, allows individual notions of the good and encourages attempts to clarify, grasp, and live up to them. But it also attends to the violences and exclusions inherent in any notion of the good and discourages unthinking attachment to one's own moral sources when encountering individuals who draw on alternative sources. Taylor is suspicious of such attempts to "gain distance from [our] own value commitments," believing that, both in principle and in practice, we simply cannot live our moral lives in such a manner (*SS,* 100). He acknowledges that allegiance to a good can result in "crushing burdens," suffering, and destruction, while hoping that this is not necessary (*SS,* 519).

Though acknowledging that the highest, most cherished goods may dominate us, Taylor insists that goods *need not* involve domination (*SS,* 100). His crucial proposition—that our deepest moral commitments need not "exact a price of self-mutilation"—is presented, again, as little more than a "hunch" (*SS*, 106–7, 519–21). But as displayed in his discussion of Foucault, Taylor has little interest in alternative, especially nonreligious or nonteleological, hunches. Nor does he display interest in practices of reflection, such as Foucault's "care of the self" and pursuit of "limit experiences," which explore hunches of dissonance, discord, and hidden injury and experience mystery and the uncanny through nonreligious prisms. Instead, Taylor encourages us to avail ourselves of those practices that may allow us to experience attunement. Thus a significant tension remains: Taylor acknowledges that his ontology is contestable while commending practices of reflection that presume it and discrediting those that do not.

Instead, Taylor persists in believing that our deepest commitments and highest ideals may be upheld without mutilation and that our conflicting ideals may be able to be reconciled. Articulation may help us deal with seemingly irreconcilable moral conflicts:

> Of course, if reconciliation is impossible, then articulacy will buy us much greater inner conflict. This might be thought a risk. But even in this case, we would have at least put an end to the stifling of the spirit and to the atrophy of so many of our spiritual sources which is the bane of modern naturalist culture. (*SS*, 107)

The outcome is uncertain. Nevertheless, Taylor's repeated emphasis is on the ways in which we should strive for reconciliation and unity, despite the costs of past failed attempts and signs that renewed attempts might be costly. In doing so, he emphasizes the costs of social fragmentation far more than the costs incurred in attempting to overcome fragmentation.

In response to Isaiah Berlin's belief that there will always be conflict between moral demands, with no formula available for resolving this conflict, Taylor explains that he is reluctant to settle for this and still seeks a mode of life, individual and social, in which conflicting demands can be reconciled.[48] Alternatively, we would do better to join Nietzsche and Hampshire in presuming that in exploring the embodied self we will encounter inner conflict, and when examining our most cherished ideals, uncover destruction and mutilation. This, however, is neither a condition to be overcome nor cause for resignation. Rather, it is *the beginning* of ethical reflection.

*

Far too many issues have been covered and comparisons made in this chapter to be captured in a single lesson. Taylor shares Arendt's appreciation of the inarticulate dimensions of the self that contribute to speech, identity, and action, and of the ways in which shared language and concerted action constitute a public realm irreducible to the individuals sustaining it, allowing a mode of being unavailable to individuals apart from it. Taylor differs most saliently from Arendt in viewing the body affirmatively, in emphasizing the important role of feeling and mood in thinking and politics, and in viewing the body teleologically, thereby sustaining his ideal of individual attunement to the world and the overcoming of alienation. Taylor shares Nietzsche's appreciation of embodiment, viewing as impoverished and misleading conceptions of thinking that see it as ideally disembodied or narrowly rational. Yet Taylor resists Nietzsche's emphasis on the considerable diversity between bodies and the recalcitrance within bodies, as this would undermine his hope for attunement and community. Taylor joins Hampshire in rejecting mind-body dualisms that sharply dichotomize accounts of subjectivity and reflection. Yet Hampshire surpasses Taylor by problematizing "nature," by exploring possibilities for *explaining* thought and action, and by pursuing a morality that incorporates deep, persistent conflict.

Taylor's most general lesson is that discussions of subjectivity and reflection that make no reference to embodiment and nature are radically insufficient. Another lesson is that assumptions and emphases regarding the body have consequences in other domains. Such assumptions and emphases, although not wholly demonstrable, are unavoidable. They influence our experience of our bodies and of society and have implications for ethics and politics. In the following chapter, we explore the extent to which alternative assumptions and emphases can allow us to experience our bodies and society differently, and can enable new ethics and politics. By this point it should be clear that, although the thickets are dense and the paths slippery, the benefits of this exploration may be considerable.

diction. See Charles Taylor, "Rationality," in *Philosophy and the Human Sciences,* 134–51; "An Iron Cage? " in *The Ethics of Authenticity* (Cambridge: Harvard University Press, 1991), 93–108; and "Explanation and Practical Reason," in *Philosophical Arguments,* 34–60. I elaborate a nonrationalist position in the following chapter.

19. Charles Taylor, "Embodied Agency," in *Merleau-Ponty: Critical Essays,* ed. Henry Pietersma (Washington, D.C.: University Press of America, 1989), 1. Hereafter cited EA. See also Charles Taylor, "Lichtung or Lebensform: Parallels between Heidegger and Wittgenstein," in *Philosophical Arguments,* 61–78.

20. Taylor wavers regarding the necessity and the possibility of providing a *transcendental* argument to convey the embodied nature of subjectivity. Compare "The Validity of Transcendental Arguments," *Philosophical Arguments,* 20–33 with EA, 17–20, and with his related conclusion that superior understandings—including, in principle, questions of how best to comprehend human affairs—have no *necessary* form but rather come down to *practical* considerations of which understanding seems best in comparison to its rivals. Charles Taylor, "Explanation and Practical Reason," in *Philosophical Arguments,* 34–60.

21. For a recent discussion of human embodiment with affinities to Taylor, see Bill Brewer, "Bodily Awareness and the Self," in *The Body and the Self,* ed. Jose Luis Bermudez, Anthony Marcel, and Naomi Eilan (Cambridge: MIT Press, 1995), 291–309. Although also seeking to undermine a Cartesian conception of the self, Brewer differs from Taylor most significantly by maintaining a sharper distinction between the mental and the physical, by focusing on certainties in awareness of one's body, and, consequently, by neglecting less-than-certain bodily sensations beneath conscious awareness.

22. A similar perspective, in the idiom of neuroscience, is found in Andy Clark, "Where Brain, Body, and World Collide," *Daedalus* 127, vol. 2 (Spring 1998): 257–80.

23. Alejo Carpentier, *The Chase,* trans. Alfred Mac Adam (New York: Noonday Press, 1989).

24. Friedrich Nietzsche, *The Gay Science,* trans. Walter Kaufmann (New York: Vintage Books, 1974), 181.

25. This does not entail that accounts of humans that make no reference to their self-understandings, or to the sense they have of their embodied grasp of the world, would themselves be adequate (EA, 15). Rather, as Rorty contends, we should pursue multiple descriptions and understandings of a single reality, none of which is complete. Rorty rejects claims, such as Taylor's usual claim, that we have access to the *ontology* of human affairs in a manner different from our access to the realm of the nonhuman. Although he denies any epistemological reason for privileging the self-understandings of subjects in our accounts of them, there is, Rorty contends, *ethical* reason for doing so, in order to display empathy. See Richard Rorty, "Method, Social Science, and Social Hope," in *Consequences of Pragmatism,* 191–210. See also Rorty's distinction of his position from that of Taylor in "Inquiry as Recontextualization: An Anti-Dualist Account

of Interpretation," in *Objectivity, Relativism, and Truth* (Cambridge: Cambridge University Press, 1991), 93–110.

26. Charles Taylor, "What's Wrong with Negative Liberty," in *Philosophy and the Human Sciences*, 213. Hereafter cited NL. Taylor is responding to the classic distinction that appears in Isaiah Berlin, "Two Concepts of Liberty," in *Four Essays on Liberty* (Oxford: Oxford University Press, 1969), 118–72.

27. Such a balance is in contrast to Taylor's claim that striving to be a certain kind of person requires us to withstand certain "craven impulses" and mere bodily appetites (WHA, 19, 22) and his fear that consumer society, manipulating our base appetites, threatens more dignified forms of freedom and autonomy. He is correct, however, to claim that personhood and freedom today must involve critical reflection on such appetites and desires. See Charles Taylor, "Alternative Futures: Legitimacy, Identity, and Alienation in Late-Twentieth-Century Canada," in *Reconciling the Solitudes: Essays on Canadian Federalism* (Montreal: McGill-Queen's University Press, 1994), 79.

28. Taylor, *Ethics of Authenticity*, 65.

29. Charles Taylor, "To Follow a Rule," in *Philosophical Arguments*, 165–80. Hereafter cited TFR.

30. See Saul A. Kripke, *Wittgenstein on Rules and Private Language* (Cambridge: Harvard University Press, 1982). See my discussion in the preceding chapter of Arendt's aversion to such a position, as it pertains to political judgment, in comparison to Richard Flathman's affinity to its emphasis on indeterminacy and, thereby, creativity.

31. See also Taylor, "Lichtung or Lebensform," 69–70. James Tully's "Wittgenstein and Political Philosophy: Understanding Practices of Critical Reflection," *Political Theory* 17, no. 2 (May 1989): 172–204, is an excellent exposition of Wittgenstein's portrait of the extensive, unquestioned background beyond the purview of particular, limited practices of critical reflection. Tully contrasts this portrait with Habermas's ideal of free and rational agreement, in which *no background* is taken for granted or is beyond the purview of reason and reflection, and with Taylor's earlier suggestion that interpretation is a constant practice rather than an exception, the need for which arises when we *do not* know how to go on. (Tully notes that Taylor now concedes this point [196]; "To Follow a Rule" and "Lichtung or Lebensform" were written since then.) Tully's argument for multiple practices of reflection—that "submission to one regime of critical reflection . . . would itself mark the end of our free and critical life" (200)—makes room for attention to embodiment as *an important* aspect of reflection, which is not to say it is the only aspect of reflection.

32. Taylor, "The Validity of Transcendental Arguments," 27–28.

33. Taylor, "Heidegger, Language, and Ecology," in *Philosophical Arguments*, 107–8, 110.

34. This is made explicit in an interview with Foucault in 1983, involving Taylor and several others, published as Michel Foucault, "Politics and Ethics: An Interview," in *The Foucault Reader*, ed. Paul Rabinow (New York: Pantheon, 1984), 377–78. Tay-

lor later identifies himself as the one who pursued an Arendtian line of questioning; see Charles Taylor, "Taylor and Foucault on Power and Freedom: A Reply," *Political Studies* 37 (1989): 278.

35. Michael Warner, "The Mass Public and the Mass Subject," in *Habermas and the Public Sphere*, ed. Craig Calhoun (Cambridge: MIT Press, 1992), 377–401; quote on 400.

36. William H. McNeill, *Keeping Together in Time: Dance and Drill in Human History* (Cambridge: Harvard University Press, 1995).

37. Taylor does note "the extraordinary development of forms of mass discipline— the regimenting of gesture and action to produce maximum effect—which begins in the eighteenth century in armies, schools, prisons, factories, and so on." Taylor, "Alternative Futures," 70.

38. Having emphasized how solidarity achieved through bodily ritual facilitates preparation for war, McNeill ends, nevertheless, by cautioning us against our present neglect of such rituals, fearing that this leads to social unravelling, unsustainable individualism, and unguided, unsatisfying lives (*Keeping Together in Time,* 152).

39. My criticisms of Taylor here resemble those made by Isaiah Berlin in his introduction to *Philosophy in an Age of Pluralism,* 1–3. I share Berlin's view of Taylor as a teleologist who believes humans to have a purpose, determined by nature and/or by God, that is discovered rather than imposed. I differ by contending that Taylor's belief that we should strive to discover our nature, if carefully qualified, has merit. The alternative is to replace teleology with an assumption of the *plasticity* of the self—as assumed by many who emphasize language and its contingency—in a way that limits alertness to violences to the self.

40. See also SIA, 64; TM, 271; "Hegel's Philosophy of Mind," in *Human Agency and Language,* 77–96.

41. Charles Taylor, "Foucault on Freedom and Truth," *Political Theory* 12, no. 2 (May 1984): 152–83.

42. Charles Taylor, "Connolly, Foucault, and Truth," *Political Theory* 13, no. 3 (August 1985): 377–85. Taylor is responding to William E. Connolly, "Taylor, Foucault, and Otherness," Political Theory 13, no. 3 (August 1985): 365–76.

43. Taylor would like to rely on *rational argument* to arbitrate between the Nietzschean view of truth as imposition and his alternative view but concedes that he has not yet provided arguments sufficient for rational arbitration. See introduction to *Human Agency and Language,* 12; and "Overcoming Epistemology," *Philosophical Arguments,* 17–19. In the meantime, alternative practices of ethical reflection may be illuminating.

44. Paul Patton, "Taylor and Foucault on Power and Freedom," *Political Studies* 37 (1989): 260–76.

45. Taylor, "Taylor and Foucault: A Reply," 278–81.

46. In a recent essay Taylor suggests that irreligious humanism can easily lead to

*anti*humanism; that Nietzsche, Bataille, and Foucault are led, in their denial of God and the transcendent and in their celebration of life, to celebrate death and destruction. Life itself can veer toward cruelty, domination, and exclusion, especially "in its moments of most exuberant affirmation" (396). Charles Taylor, "The Immanent Counter-Enlightenment," in *Canadian Political Philosophy: Contemporary Reflections,* ed. Ronald Beiner and Wayne Norman (Oxford: Oxford University Press, 2001), 386–400. Similar reservations are expressed in Hampshire's reading of Sade.

47.   Quentin Skinner contends that the historical record gives reason to fear Christianity, as it has been accompanied so often by war and persecution, and that atheists can affirm humanity at least as much as can theists; see "Modernity and Disenchantment: Some Historical Reflections," in *Philosophy in an Age of Pluralism,* 37-48. Taylor responds: "I have a hunch that there is a scale of affirmation of humanity by God which cannot be matched by humans rejecting God. But I am far from having proof." "Reply and Re-articulation," in *Philosophy in an Age of Pluralism,* 226.

48.   Taylor, "Reply and Re-articulation," 214.

3

THE CORPOREALITY OF THOUGHT

THE PRIMACY OF THE BODY IN FRIEDRICH NIETZSCHE

> Philosophy has succeeded, not without a struggle, in freeing itself from its obsession with the soul, only to find itself landed with something still more mysterious and captivating: the fact of Man's bodiliness.
> —Friedrich Nietzsche

References and allusions to the body abound in Nietzsche's texts. For example, in *Twilight of the Idols* we read of the animality of philosophy, the apes of ideals, the ugly face of Socrates, the need to bite off the head of bad conscience, the usefulness of the nose, the narcotic of Christianity, the sickness of the supposedly wise, the appetite for dialectic, the eroticism of argument, the disarray of instinct, the darkness of desires, the play and counterplay of organs, the metabolism of virtue, the taming of beasts, the breeding of men, the castration of priests, weakness, hunger, injury, pain, exhaustion, and the importance of eating well.[1]

In *The Human Condition* Arendt states, without elaboration, that Nietzsche revaluated "the sensual and natural as against the supersensual and supernatural," that he revaluated the metaphysical in terms of the physical.[2] Nietzsche did seek to invert hierarchies central to much of philosophy and religion—the subordination of body to soul, of flesh to spirit, of the worldly to the afterworld, of cities of men to the city of God—hierarchies that persist. In countless passages Nietzsche urges us to choose passion over reason, instinct over morality, physiological diagnosis over philosophical analysis, and action over contemplation. However, I shall pursue slightly different, more subtle strands in Nietzsche's writings. Although Nietzsche emphasizes the body and those elements of life associated with it, such as passion, feeling, sensuality, appetite, desire, drive, instinct, posture, and mood, ultimately he strives for *the corporeality of thought*—that is, tension, cooperation, and complementarity between that classified as "mind" and "body." To the extent that this dualism is retained—and it may have to be, since it is embedded in our grammar, and for this reason Nietzsche is forced to use terms he knows to be inadequate and unstable—he wishes to reconfigure it. In a reconfigured dualism, neither mind nor body governs, but rather their complex interactions are attended to while a delicate reciprocity is maintained. Such careful, ongoing attention to the corporeality of thought is not easy, but Nietzsche viewed sustaining it, including in his own life and work, as critically important.

Elaborating Nietzsche's belief in the primacy of the body for selfhood and thinking, and the implications of this for ethics and politics, distinguishes Arendt's ambivalence toward the body from a stance far less ambivalent. In doing so, it begins to explain her ambivalence toward Nietzsche. It also supports my criticisms of Taylor, particularly regarding his teleological conception of the embodied self and his attachment to the transcendental and the spiritual, suggesting an alternative that I continue to develop in the next chapter.

Less than Arendt, and far less than Taylor, does Nietzsche provide systematic arguments or consistent formulations. His writings resist summary, as they are not entirely unified but rather contain strongly conflicting tendencies and dissenting voices. Indeed, such tensions and dissonances within his thinking are consistent with his *image of thought* and with his belief that selfhood and thinking, at their best, incorporate a number of perspectives and harbor plurality, contradiction, and becoming.[3] To reduce his thinking to neat formulas or dispassionate arguments would domesticate Nietzsche. Nevertheless, across his writings, Nietzsche *does* suggest certain formulations, a number of which I tease out and reconstruct. The challenge is to do so without losing (at least not all of) the subtlety and affective power of his writings. By placing Nietzsche's insights and formulations alongside those of other thinkers, the tension and dissonance necessary for thinking are maintained.[4]

THE WORLD AND THINKING

Nietzsche's discussions of the body are bound up with his discussions of the world and of thinking itself. The body serves as a nexus for these concerns, as it is both object and subject, of the world and knower of the world.[5] Nietzsche's suppositions regarding the character of the world underlie those regarding the body and stem from his own experience of the world and of his body. A few themes require summary.

Nietzsche's ontology and epistemology entail that our ability to know the world is limited. This limitation arises from the character of the world and from our capacities for knowing. He rejects metaphysical and teleological conceptions of nature, which presume the world to have a stable structure or essential purpose to be captured in our accounts of it. Instead, he offers a conception—or, more precisely, *explores a supposition*—of the world. "And do you know what 'the world' is to me? Shall I show it to you in my mirror? This world: a monster of energy, without beginning, without end."[6] The statement is suppositional and perspectival —"what 'the world' is *to me*"—and our grasp of the world is mediated, as we perceive it indirectly through mirrors. Nietzsche's is a world of plurality and contradiction rather than unity and harmony, flux and becoming rather than stasis and eternal being, depth and opacity rather than shallowness and transparency, accident and chance rather than purpose and necessity.[7]

Indeed, the fundamental, costly mistake of metaphysics—the assumption that beneath transience lies permanence, that "at bottom everything stands still"—is unsettled when we look no further than the volatility and impermanence of our own bodies (*TSZ*, 126, 201). Such assumptions of permanence have harmful ethical and political implications; they are not only mistaken but also "misanthropic," at odds with individual creativity and becoming (*TSZ*, 86–87). Moreover, they have led philosophers (most notably Plato) to denigrate the body, to see the senses as unreliable and inadequate for capturing the essence of being beneath the surface of becoming.

Philosophers who esteem reason, conceived as independent of the senses, view the senses as "*so immoral as well,* it is they which deceive us about the *real* world. . . . And away . . . with the *body,* that pitiable *idée fixe* of the senses!" (*TI,* 45).

The "good man," like the philosopher, wants attunement with the world and "believes in the possibility of getting to the bottom of things. For why should the world deceive him?"[8] Yet the world always deceives us, to the extent that our accounts of it, unavoidably, understate its singularity, plurality, and becoming. The world is never fully apprehended, its shadowy recesses never fully illuminated, as our accounts of it cannot attend to all of its dimensions.[9] In a manner reminiscent of Hobbes's Leviathan, whose first act and supreme power is to assign names, Nietzsche stresses the power of language, of organizing the world through concepts and categories, demarcations and distinctions.[10]

Although its practitioners are seldom conscious of it, a "will to truth" is also a "will to power." It is a

> will to the thinkability of all beings . . . to make all being thinkable, for you doubt with well-founded suspicion that it is already thinkable. But it shall yield and bend for you. Thus your will wants it. It shall become smooth and serve the spirit as its mirror and reflection. (*TSZ,* 113)

Recall Arendt's conclusion, following Jaspers, that the task of thinking is not to reduce being to the "thinkable" but instead "'to aggravate . . . [its] unthinkability.'" Arendt emphasizes the unthinkability of being without exploring the implications of this for the body. Yet here Nietzsche suggests that the body itself is, in important respects, unthinkable. For it is "will" and "spirit" (traditionally conceived as both inhabiting the body and distinct from it, a view he criticizes) that want the body to be transparent, to yield and bend, to be smooth and serving. In contrast, to aggravate the body's unthinkability is to attend to that which exceeds the scope of will and reason, which is not always smooth and serving.

Wisdom involves chastening the will to truth and recognizing the limits of will and reason. It involves aggravating the unthinkability of being and, in doing so, acknowledging the limits to knowledge (*TI,* 33). In this regard, the will to truth itself becomes *a problem*—"the value of truth must for once be experimentally *called into question.*" "[W]hat meaning would *our* whole being possess if . . . the will to truth becomes conscious of itself as a *problem?*" (*GM*, 153, 161). In later sections of this chapter we shall pursue this suggestion—that our lives take on new tones when the will to truth remains a problem and when wisdom is seen as thoughtful, experimental living, including reflection on our bodies and their relation to knowing.[11]

PERSPECTIVE AND EVALUATION

Central to Nietzsche's epistemology are his beliefs that knowledge is perspectival and embodied. Knowledge is perspectival in large part *because* it is embodied. As discussed above, our accounts of the world are inherently limited, and alternative accounts are in other respects limited. Consequently, rather than futile attempts at impartiality or comprehensiveness, or pretensions of disinterestedness, we should "employ a *variety* of perspectives and affective interpretations in the service of knowledge" (*GM*, 119). Two broad claims are discernible in this statement. The first regards the importance of acknowledging the limited vantage point of any perspective. We can respond to this limitation by striving to inhabit multiple vantage points, identifying vantage points we are unable to inhabit, and being receptive to perspectives flowing from them.

The second claim regards the contribution of affect to perspective. Our particular affects particularize our perspective, a genuine plurality of perspectives requires a plurality of affects, and the irreducible plurality of affects entails the irreducible plurality of perspectives.[12]

In sum:

There is *only* a perspective seeing, *only* a perspective 'knowing'; and the *more* affects we allow to speak about one thing, the more eyes, different eyes, we can use to observe one thing, the more complete will our 'concept' of this thing, our 'objectivity,' be. But to eliminate the will altogether, to suspend each and every affect, supposing we were capable of this—what would that mean but to *castrate* the intellect? (*GM*, 119)

We should enlist a multiplicity of limited perspectives rather than striving for a single, unlimited perspective. And we must prepare ourselves for the demands of thinking, preparation that involves attending to and modifying affect.

The knowing subject—situated, myopic, affective, and short-lived—is crucially embodied. Its body influences its acquisition of knowledge, and, as I shall soon discuss, acquiring knowledge influences its body, which complicates things greatly. In *Ecce Homo,* Nietzsche reflects on his life and thought and in order to do so discusses his physical health and development, his habits of daily living, and the complex relation of each of these to his thinking. New activity and experiences enabled new thinking, and new thinking enabled new activity and experiences. For example, he wrote *The Dawn* during a period of intense physical discomfort, allowing a "clarity *par excellence*" that enabled him to think through matters in a manner unavailable to him in his earlier state (*EH,* 222–23). Appreciating and modifying his bodily states allowed advances in thinking. He became subtler in his "organs of observation," learning to reverse perspectives and reevaluate values by gaining familiarity with and modulating affect and instinct (*EH,* 223).

The rootedness of thinking in the body makes condemnations of life suspect, as they often stem from an unhealthy life. This paradox—that values arise out of life, that they reflect a particular state of life, and therefore lack the detachment needed to appraise life—is expressed concisely in a chapter in *Twilight of the Idols* entitled "Morality as Anti-Nature":

> [A] condemnation of life by the living is after all no more than the symptom of a certain kind of life . . . One would have to be situated *outside* life, and on the other hand to know it as thoroughly as any, as many, as all who have experienced it, to be permitted to touch on the problem of the *value* of life. . . . When we speak of values we do so under the inspiration and from the perspective of life: *life itself evaluates through us when we establish values."* (*TI,* 55, final emphasis mine)

Those who are healthy are led to presume the value of life, while those who are unhealthy are led to denigrate life. The value of life is not a problem. Rather, the problem is the conditions of life that discourage some from creating value. Material conditions and bodily states are said to give rise not just to negative evaluations but to *every* evaluation.[13] In one of his strongest formulations, "Our most sacred convictions, the unchanging elements in our supreme values, are judgments of our muscles" (*WP*, sec. 314). Consequently, reevaluation and overcoming of values, especially of supreme values, involves attention to the conditions of life and bodily states sustaining these values.[14]

The corporeality of thought is further complicated by the fact that not only does the body influence evaluation, but also evaluation influences the body. We embody inherited evaluations. As a result, our reflection on them is influenced, paradoxically, by bodily dispositions that are a product, in part, of these inherited evaluations. As Zarathustra explains to his disciples, "all these mistakes [of spirit and virtue] still dwell in our body . . . much ignorance and error have become body within us" (*TSZ*, 77). Foucault's most explicit discussion of Nietzsche centers on this complexity: "Historical descent attaches itself to the body. It inscribes itself in the nervous system, in temperament, in the digestive apparatus; it appears in faulty respiration, in improper diets, in the debilitated and prostrate body of those ancestors who committed errors."[15] Foucault's genealogies may be seen, then, as striving to expose the contingency of inherited instincts and affects and to unsettle current dispositions and identities, thereby allowing new values and possibilities for living.

Consider, for example, the *gut reaction* a person might have to masculine women or feminine men in a culture that stigmatizes these. If such gut reactions are strong enough, presumptions concerning feminine women and masculine men may sustain this person's supreme values and be less questioned than passed over in reflection. Such reactions, and their implicit evaluations and appraisals, are fundamental to thinking and acting.[16] In short, we are trapped in a circle in which the bodily dispositions involved in our thinking often support the very evaluations that we wish to reconsider. There does not appear to be any means of raising ourselves above this, short of introducing metaphysical or theological assumptions likely to be even more problematical. Thinking requires, nevertheless, attention to the bodily dispositions stemming from inherited evaluations, since these dispositions may be influencing and limiting our thinking in ways of which we are unaware.

We acknowledge, then, the contributions of disposition and affect to thinking but also remain critical of them, as they often limit our thinking. Our criticism of disposition and affect may be inspired by certain values and commitments or by other contrary, subordinate, or inchoate dispositions and affects. Ethics thus involves modifying evaluations by attending to disposition and affect and, by doing so, achieving a new configuration of evaluation, disposition, and affect. Ideally, this new configuration will be subjected, periodically, to additional rounds of such multifaceted reflection. This approaches Hampshire's portrait of the *multiple* sites for intervening in thinking and feeling and the resultant, often unexpected "feed-back" from such interventions. Such interventions alter one's body in its faculties and capacities, giving rise to new thoughts, feelings, questions, possibilities, and limits. Changes in one's body may enable new thinking, and new thinking may enable changes in one's body.

These issues are made vivid in André Gide's novel *The Immoralist*, which one translator rightly remarks could as well have been entitled "toward a genealogy of morals." In it, the protagonist, Michel, through new bodily activity and experiences, gradually discovers his "unsuspected faculties" and advances toward "a richer, fuller life." This is in response to being told that "[a] man has to choose. What matters is to know what he wants. . . . Of the thousand forms of life, each of us can know only one." Michel replies: "But I've grown. And now my happiness is too tight for me. Sometimes I'm almost strangled by it."[17] New activity and experiences allow Michel to loosen his previously unquestioned form of life.

Regrettably, instead of attending to the affective dimensions of thinking, many attempt to excise these dimensions, to treat the body as a distraction. Nietzsche believes this to be deeply mistaken. Rather, what is needed in thinking is offered, suggestively, as "the gentle radiation of a rich animality" into moral domains (*TI,* 54). Thinking, at its best, involves not the fiction of disembodiment but rather attention to the embodied nature of thinking.[18] Yet even when this is done, any individual's capacity for reflection and evaluation remains limited, partly as a result of the limitations of his or her body and *particular* affects and dispositions. Since no individual can embody all values, maintain all dispositions, or be familiar with all affects, a thorough reevaluation of values *exceeds the bodily capacities* of any individual. "For the task of a *reevaluation of all values* more capacities may have been needed than have ever dwelt together in a single individual—above all, even contrary capacities that had to be kept from disturbing and destroying one another" (*EH*, 254).

In the above respects, then, perspective and evaluation are inherently embodied. Making sense of the world requires making sense of one's body, since one's grasp of the world is inseparable from one's embodiment. Thinking is bodily, and one of the most important objects of knowledge is one's body. This alone establishes the importance of the body for selfhood and thinking. We shall return to Nietzsche's discussions of what I have termed the corporeality of thought, but first his conception of the self must be made more explicit.

BODY AND SOUL

In discussing Nietzsche's supposition of the character of the world and of the body, the bodily basis of thinking, and the influence of knowledge on the body, we have begun to formulate his conception of the self. We may now consider further the self's configuration, origins, and possibilities. Nietzsche's conception of the self differs fundamentally from what he saw as the dominant conception in his time, of which more than traces remain today. Elaborating Nietzsche's conception introduces an alternative to Arendt's and Taylor's respective conceptions and lays the groundwork for discussion of that of Hampshire. In doing so, it focuses on that which dispensing with the soul requires—the fact of human bodiliness.

Nietzsche rejects Christianity's dualism of body and soul, which privileges the afterworld over the world, and philosophy's dualism of body and mind, which variously conceives of the mind as independent of the body and gives primacy to consciousness. Somewhat less clearly, he seems unsatisfied not only with conceptions of the self such as Taylor's, in which an authentic core is to be expressed, but also with conceptions such as Rorty's, in which the self possesses a plasticity allowing unconstrained creation and recreation. His conception lies somewhere between these, as the depths of the self are to be explored and to some extent expressed, and its fundamental attributes modified and in some instances overcome. In brief, the self is presented as a complex organization of the body, characterized by its depth, opacities, and internal tensions and authorities. The self is the body organized—never securely or exhaustively—by language, reason, and morality, by political settlements and cultural conventions.

Nietzsche's most accessible discussion of the body and the self is found in successive sections in *Thus Spoke Zarathustra* entitled "On the Afterworldly" and "On the Despisers of the Body." Here Zarathustra begins with a number of the points discussed above—the bodily bases of evaluation and how bodily suffering leads to negative evaluations of life and of the body:

> [I]t was the body that despaired of the body and touched the ultimate walls with the fingers of a deluded spirit. . . . [I]t was the body that despaired of the earth and heard the belly of being speak to it. It wanted to crash through these walls with its head, and not only with its head—over there to 'that world' . . . that dehumanized inhuman world which is a heavenly nothing. (*TSZ*, 31–32)

Bodily suffering and limitation lead many to invent the spirit (a "*deluded* spirit") as something to be relieved of the body, or at least of its inconveniences. The spirit wants to crash through the walls of limitation and mortality into the afterworld. Such a disembodied, immortal, limitless world would be empty, devoid of meaning, "a heavenly nothing." Zarathustra advises, instead, to "no longer bury one's head in the sand of heavenly things, but to bear it freely, an earthly head, which creates a new meaning for the earth" (*TSZ*, 32). And we should "[l]isten . . . to the voice of the healthy body: that is a more honest and purer voice. . . . [I]t speaks of the meaning of the earth" (*TSZ*, 33).

Despairing of the body and longing for a "dehumanized inhuman" world can be observed today. A recent, extreme instance was the suicide of Marshall Applewhite and thirty-eight of his followers in California. Applewhite sought early in life to dispense with his homosexual desires, attempting abstinence, then admitting himself to a psychiatric hospital to be cured, then attempting to limit himself to platonic relationships, then having himself castrated, then founding a religion in which members practiced celibacy and often elected castration, then orchestrating a mass suicide. Observers described Applewhite as a man who found his own body to be a "crushing disappointment," who hoped that he could leave his body and, in heaven, find another.[19]

We are taught to say, as Applewhite himself taught, "'Body am I, and soul.'" "But the awakened and knowing say: body am I entirely, and nothing else; and *soul is only a word for something about the body*" (*TSZ*, 34, emphasis mine).[20] Being the body entirely and nothing else is not so limiting, as it would be if the body were characterized by a small number of simple needs and wants, with little variance across individuals, cultures, or times. But Nietzsche does not believe this to be the case. Far from it, "[t]he body is a great reason, a plurality with one sense, a war and a peace, a herd and a shepherd" (*TSZ*, 34). Each body is itself a *polity*—a complex social structure and political settlement comprised of reason and passions, conflict and consensus, and leaders, followers, and dissidents. Within each individual, residing in part beneath consciousness, are multiple, often contradictory passions, desires, needs, inclinations, aversions, inhibitions, alliances, and settlements.[21]

Zarathustra proceeds to explain, in a less clear passage, the internal configuration of the self and some of its principal features. "An instrument of your body is also your little reason," serving but not pervading the self (*TSZ*, 34). Ego, which mistakenly understands itself as governing the self, is actually a subordinate, limited constituent within the self (*TSZ*, 35). The self, then, is not distinct from, but is an organization of, the body: "Behind your thoughts and feelings . . . there stands a mighty ruler, an unknown sage—whose name is self. In your body he dwells; he is your body" (*TSZ*, 34). Soul, mind, will, reason, and ego are not, then, independent of the body, or somehow less bodily, but are features of an organized body, a self. Selfhood is a mode of embodiment characterized by such organizational complexity.

Given its abundance and complexity, the body *exceeds* identity, possessing attributes and capacities that are subordinated, occluded, or viewed as less essential to us. Identity is more selective and narrow, consisting of those aspects of the self that are foregrounded, willfully and confidently presented as "I" (*TSZ*, 34). Such abundance and complexity of the self contribute to the fluidity of identity, allowing successive presentations to others that accentuate select aspects of oneself.[22]

Self-presentation and expression are seldom sufficient, as the idiosyncrasy and singularity of our inner states prevent their capture in a common language. Rarely do our public identities correspond fully to our inner dispositions, as the former are selections and translations of the latter. "Our true experiences are not garrulous. They could not communicate themselves if they wanted to: they lack words. . . . The speaker has already *vulgarized* himself by speaking" (*TI*, 94). Thus, paradoxically, individuality is enacted in a social medium that limits individuation. Arendt is no doubt drawing on these themes in viewing identity as a selective presentation of inner dispositions, a selection of what is "fit" to appear. Yet Arendt's emphasis is contrary to Nietzsche's, as she sees self-presentation as far more rich and varied than inner life. For Nietzsche, the richness and abundance of our inner lives inspire and sustain our public identities.

Having discussed the primacy of the body, we must mention Nietzsche's emphasis on the body's opacities. In his notebooks he asks:

> What does man actually know about himself? Is he, indeed, ever able to perceive himself completely, as if laid out in a lighted display case? Does nature not conceal most things from him—even concerning his own body—in order to confine and lock him within a proud, deceptive consciousness, aloof from the coils of the bowels, the rapid flow of the bloodstream, and the intricate quivering of the fibers![23]

This passage needs to be qualified today, as technologies such as magnetic resonance imaging *do* allow us to lay ourselves out in a lighted display case. It might be read now to suggest that, even when so laid out, the body retains a degree of elusiveness and opacity, as fears, desires, moods, anxieties, and the like, although bodily, are not subject to representation in the way simpler bodily states are.[24] This converges with Taylor's contention that certain dimensions of the embodied self are inherently subjective and not susceptible to objective accounts, and with Hampshire's arguments for the inherent elusiveness of inner states.

Yet such opacities of the self should not be assumed to be permanent. Imagine how greatly it would affect individual subjectivity if one could check the level of certain chemicals in one's bloodstream when feeling the onset of a particular mood as easily as one can check blood sugar level when feeling the onset of fatigue. This knowledge would reconfigure subjectivity and add complexity to thinking. Such possibilities (likely to be realized) keep us from being confined within a "proud, deceptive consciousness," making subjectivity less confining and more modest.

CULTURE AND MORALITY

Language, reason, culture, and morality begin as impositions on the body that then become part of it, not as ornaments or appendages, but as fundamental features. They are, in one respect, foreign to the body and counter to life, but are also deeply installed in the body, organizing and enabling life. Nietzsche refrains, however, from seeing language, reason, culture, and morality as wholly comprising or fully pervading the self, as going all the way down.[25]

Words and values only partly constitute the self, as the self is neither independent of, nor reducible to, them. "We are presented with grave words and values almost from the cradle"; man "carries on his shoulders too much that is alien to him. Like a camel, he kneels down and lets himself be well loaded. . . . [H]e loads too many *alien* grave words and values on himself" (*TSZ*, 193). At the beginning of *Zarathustra* the well-loaded camel is presented as the lowest stage of individual development, succeeded by the lion and then by the child, who has not yet been loaded down with society's words and values (*TSZ*, 25–27). The suggestion, then, is that *all* words and values are to some extent alien to us, that they are always inadequate, not only enabling us but also weighing us down, remaining in tension with aspects of ourselves. Below we discuss the implications of this suggestion for thinking and social arrangements. In the chapter to follow, we discuss the practices of reflection, beyond those commended by Taylor, by which this suggestion can be pursued, and the means by which individuals can identify the words and values most alien to them and loading them down.

Within his general account of the self, Nietzsche emphasizes that understanding any *particular* configuration requires a historical account.

Indeed, his genealogies of morality and examinations of moral psychology include extensive discussion of historical operations on the body, of its linguistic and cultural penetration and political organization. Through such operations, the body has been organized and stabilized to become a subject and a responsible agent. The body's (especially certain bodies') lack of predisposition to these forms makes such operations arduous, painful, and never entirely successful. Moreover, the transition from nature to society cannot be viewed as wholly conscious or volitional, as new formations of consciousness and volition are themselves products of this transition.[26]

Nietzsche frequently presents his accounts in evolutionary terms, speaking of the "animal" in us that has been subdued by consciousness and civilization. He writes, for example, of the earlier, noble races whose members periodically stepped outside of society, temporarily resuming their status as "uncaged beasts of prey," compensating themselves for "the tension engendered by protracted confinement and enclosure within the peace of society" (*GM*, 40). Such releases are necessary, as "this hidden core needs to erupt from time to time, the animal has to get out again and go back to the wilderness" (*GM*, 41). Nietzsche suggests that, at base, "the *meaning of all culture* is the reduction of the beast of prey 'man' to a tame and civilized animal, a *domestic animal*" (*GM*, 42).

If culture serves to tame and reconstitute men and women, then the "instincts of reaction and *ressentiment*," which overthrew the noble races, prohibiting their primal furloughs, are themselves "the actual *instruments of culture*" (*GM*, 42). That is, some instincts—those dispositions and drives counter to life—are artifacts of stifling culture that in turn serve these cultures. Such culturally induced instincts have led us to become ashamed of our more basic instincts, contributing to "the *regression* of mankind" (*GM*, 43). This is not an opposition between natural instinct and culture, as instinct is seen as a mixture of nature and culture. Rather, our supreme values, such as responsibility, though initially impositions, have "penetrated to the profoundest depths and become instinct" (*GM*, 60).

Pivotal in this reorganization of the self, in which the animal is subdued and inhibitions reign, in which we come to be calculable, regular, uniform, and dependable, is the convention of promising. This transition amounts to

> the most fundamental change [man] ever experienced—that change which
> occurred when he found himself finally enclosed within the walls of society and
> of peace. . . . [S]uddenly all their instincts were disvalued and 'suspended'. . . .
> [T]hese unfortunate creatures, they were reduced to their 'consciousness,' their
> weakest and most fallible organ! . . . [A]t the same time the old instincts had not
> suddenly ceased to make their usual demands! Only it was hardly or rarely pos-
> sible to humor them: as a rule they had to seek new, and, as it were, subterranean
> gratifications. (*GM*, 84)

This transition "forcibly confined [men] to the oppressive narrowness and
punctiliousness of custom, impatiently lacerated, persecuted, gnawed at";
it led to an "animal that rubbed itself raw against the bars of its cage as one
tried to 'tame' it" (*GM*, 85). The ascetic priest sought to manage and
deploy human drives. But the ascetic ideal of "life *against* life" is a physiological contradiction, as it is counter to the "deepest instincts of life"
(*GM*, 120–21, 139–41).[27] The challenge, then, is to modify those
instincts that are most counter to life.

Such work on the self is always occurring. As the Greeks are said to have
known best, in order to achieve excellence or beauty

> a mere disciplining of thoughts and feelings is virtually nothing . . . one first has
> to convince the body. . . . [I]n two or three generations everything is already
> internalized. It is decisive for the fortune of nations and of mankind that one
> should inaugurate culture in the right place—not in the 'soul'; . . . the right place
> is the body, demeanor, diet, physiology: the rest follows. (*TI*, 112)

The claim is that every social order, in order to be sustained, must be
inaugurated in the bodies of subjects. Given Nietzsche's other remarks, it
must be added that the body itself limits the stability of any inauguration.
It requires strenuous effort to lodge certain values, postures, and rhythms
in the body, and once set, they become entrenched and are difficult to
dislodge. This is especially the case for the supreme values and fundamental assumptions of any social order, for the crucial underpinnings
that must remain securely in place, insulated from denial and doubt.

Such values and assumptions are installed in individuals through *"mnemotechnics"*—painful rituals and "repulsive mutilations." "[A] few ideas are to be rendered inextinguishable, ever-present, unforgettable, 'fixed,' with the aim of hypnotising the entire nervous and intellectual system, . . . freeing these ideas from the competition of all other ideas, so as to make them 'unforgettable'" (*GM*, 61). Rituals and techniques ingrain in each member of society "five or six 'I will not's'" that go unquestioned (*GM*, 62).

Such rituals and techniques are most vivid when exaggerated in fiction, such as Kafka's "In the Penal Colony," in which a condemned man has the commandment that he violated written into his flesh. An officer explains: "It would be no use informing him [of our judgment]. He's going to experience it on his body anyway." Through such a procedure "[e]ven the stupidest man is . . . enlightened."[28] Actual instances of fixing ideas through politically sanctioned rituals involving bodily practices are elucidated in social theorist Paul Connerton's *How Societies Remember.* "Every group . . . will entrust to bodily automatisms the values and categories which they are most anxious to conserve. They will know how well the past can be kept in mind by a habitual memory sedimented in the body."[29] Sedimentation in the body, Connerton argues, helps account for the inertia of social structures, for the noncognitive and nonsymbolic underpinnings of sanctioned cognition and symbols.

In one of his most concise discussions of the political organization of the self, Nietzsche narrates the pivotal role of Socrates.[30] Socrates is said to have facilitated the transition from an era of Homeric instinct and Dionysian expression to one of reason and decadence. At base, Socratic reason sought to master instinct, and Athenian decadence followed its denial of life. This new governance by reason rested on the moral imperative of rationality, captured in Socrates' "bizarrest of equations," that reason was equivalent to virtue and happiness (*TI*, 41).

Socrates believed this new equation to be necessary, since the cultural order of Athens was disappearing, with authority degenerating and instincts in disarray. Reason was then introduced as the new master in this reconsolidation of the self, as "a *counter-tyrant* who is stronger" than opposing instincts. Socrates, himself acutely suffering an anarchy of instincts, typified the successful organization of a reasonable self, gaining mastery over every "evil lust" (*TI*, 43). Following Socrates' reception, "dark desires" were permanently countered by the harsh "daylight of reason," with thinking coming to be seen as bright and cold (*TI*, 43).

Socrates' imperative of rationality returns us to our discussion of thinking. To confine thinking to rational consciousness, to fail to attend to its less rational and less conscious dimensions, is to be less thoughtful. It risks being so because when confined to the narrow terrain of the conscious, the rational, and the articulate, essential elements of thinking are ignored.[31] Indeed, Socratic argument, that "pitiless instrument" that demands articulate reasons for every commitment, "devitalizes the opponent's intellect" (*TI*, 42). It tyrannizes one's opponent, putting her on the defensive and pressing her to acquiesce, since seldom can she provide solely rational justification for her commitments. And in such interrogation, the mood and sensibility underlying her commitments, as well as those of her opponent, remain unexamined. In this respect—contrary to the aspirations of critical rationalism—exclusively rational engagement can be *un*critical, it can be shallow and dogmatic, complacent and unquestioning, bullying and impatient. Moreover, such engagement is often ineffective, since that which one adopts *without* reasons—affect, mood, disposition—often cannot be challenged *with* reasons (*TI*, 42–43).[32]

At base, the introduction of Socratic dialectics marked a change not in arguments or ideas but in "taste," in which the previous, nobler taste was defeated (*TI*, 41). And as Zarathustra explains, "all of life is a dispute over taste and tasting. Taste—that is at the same time weight and scales and weigher; and woe unto all the living that would live without disputes over weights and scales and weighers!" (*TSZ*, 117). Not to subject taste to consideration and criticism is to neglect fundamental dimensions of ethical value. Attention only to intellectual developments and attempts to counteract them through narrowly intellectual means are inadequate. This itself sheds light on Nietzsche's style of writing, which employs rhetorical flair, disturbing imagery, and personal attack to variously incite, arouse, provoke, frighten, entertain, coax, seduce, and bewilder his readers. Given the perdurance of the tendencies and traditions he wishes to unsettle, calm, dispassionate argument would almost certainly be inadequate.[33]

Rather, intellectual change itself often requires new physical activity. Ethics involves such work on the self, including attention to the political and cultural operations on the body and to the activities of daily living. This is especially important for those who aspire to individuality—for a life that does not merely perpetuate one's inherited morality and culture but rather attempts to modify or depart from them. Transformation—ethical and political, of culture and of ourselves—is not merely an intellectual process but must go deeper, engaging and modifying affect, mood, desire, and disposition. "We are growing more Greek by the day; at first, as is only fair, in concepts and evaluations, as Hellenizing ghosts, as it were; but one day, let us hope, also in our *bodies!*" (*WP,* sec. 419).

PATHS OF LIFE

We have seen that for Nietzsche the unthinkability of being extends to certain aspects of embodiment; that perspective and evaluation are embodied and affective; that the self is an artifact of culture composed in part of material preceding culture; and that not only concepts and arguments but also affect, mood, disposition, and passions must be challenged and modified. We may end by considering the extent to which dissonant elements and unrealized capacities of the body can be explored; differences in individual constitution and inclination accommodated; and the material and physical conditions of thinking, and its implication in practices, routines, and habits of daily living, require attention.

Nietzsche urges, in contrast to a deep vein in Taylor, that rather than strive for social unity we acknowledge individual differences and the multiplicity of individual ends, and accommodate them to the greatest extent feasible. In his implicit criticisms of Aristotle, Nietzsche challenges teleological conceptions of human development, in which individual flourishing consists of aspiring to preestablished ends. Zarathustra similarly criticizes the priestly attempt to "[drive] their herd over . . . a single path" (*TSZ*, 92). Presumption of the diversity and unrealized possibilities of individual bodies underlies Nietzsche's denial of a teleology of development. Given bodily diversity and possibilities, insistence on a single path neglects or forecloses, somewhat arbitrarily, alternative paths.[34]

Insisting on one or two paths results, unavoidably, in those individuals who stray from these paths being "thrust out, as unworthy, as a source of pollution" (*TI*, 110). Yet outside set paths of life, Zarathustra explains, lie "a thousand paths that have never yet been trodden—a thousand healths and hidden isles of life" (*TSZ*, 77). Discovering untrodden paths of life, unfamiliar healths of our bodies, and hidden isles of life involves reevaluation of practices and values. And it requires a political culture of deep pluralism, with opportunities for such inquiry and experimentation.

For all of its nuance and complexity, Martha Nussbaum's effort to resurrect a modest Aristotelian essentialism risks herding us over a single path.[35] Contending that the current emphasis on cultural diversity has gone too far, eclipsing recognition of shared humanity and undermining the bases for transcultural judgment, Nussbaum develops a "thick vague theory of the good" (214). She compiles a list of items constituting "what seems to be part of any life that we will count as a human life" (216), including aversion to death, pain, and hunger; sexual desire; the wish to move about; reliance on reason to plan and manage one's life; appreciation of the beauty and wonder of nature; and play. The majority of humans today probably conform to most of these items, but each also admits of numerous individual and civilizational exceptions (e.g., daredevils, masochists, crash dieters, celibates, provincials, spendthrifts, thrill seekers, Manhattanites, and Stoics). To view such nonconformists as less than fully human, as Nussbaum's theory cannot avoid doing, is likely to give rise to condescending, coercive, or abusive treatment of them.[36]

Nietzsche counters even such modest essentialist claims by insisting that "there is no health as such, and all attempts to define a thing that way have been wretched failures. Even the determination of what is healthy for your *body* depends on your goal, your horizon, your energies, your impulses, your errors, and above all the ideals and phantasms of your soul. Thus there are innumerable healths of the body" (*GS*, 176–77). Whereas moralists deny the "wealth of types," strong ages embrace diversity and allow multiple paths (*TI*, 56, 102). One means of allowing a wealth of types is to maintain a society with enough cultures and subcultures, enough nooks and crannies, so that individuals can gravitate toward those that they find more agreeable and accommodating. Another, complementary means is to cultivate an ethic of greater openness to subordinate elements of society and of ourselves. Such attention to subordinate elements in society and in oneself, and to unusual bodies and unrealized possibilities of one's body, is part of a genuine reevaluation of values.[37] In the next chapter I consider the ways in which Nietzsche may overstate the diversity of needs and the extent to which deep pluralism can coexist with tentative identification of basic needs.

Attention to the body, in which we come to understand, appreciate, and modify various aspects of ourselves, is not a single event. Rather, it permeates our daily lives. Nietzsche contends, however, that this receives far too little emphasis in philosophy—in its image of thought and its corresponding ideals for thinking and education. Far more important than the theologian's concern for the salvation of the soul and classical education's focus on idealism is "the question of *nutrition*" (*EH*, 237). Reflecting on his own life and work, Nietzsche discusses their imbrication in his habits and activities of living, recounting how he gradually discovered, after years of trial and error, how various foods affected him, and how his affinity or aversion to various cultures involved his reaction to their lifestyles and patterns of consumption. For example, although he realized this late, he concluded, "Alcohol is bad for me: a single glass of wine or beer in one day is quite sufficient to turn my life into a vale of misery" (*EH*, 238). Alcohol had deleterious effects on his mood, and thus on his thinking, something he realized after experimenting with consumption and sensing the corresponding effects. The point is not to prescribe that the rest of us follow suit, as "moralists" would prescribe, but that we discover what seems best for us.

Nobody functions equally well in every setting. A mistaken choice in this regard can estrange one from one's task:

> [T]he effects of climate and weather are familiar to me from long experience and I take readings from myself as from a very subtle instrument. . . . I reflect with horror on the *dismal* fact that my life, except for the last ten years . . . was spent entirely in the wrong places that were nothing short of *forbidden* to me . . . so many disastrous places for my physiology. (EH, 241)

It was "the ignorance *in physiologicis*—that damned 'idealism'—that was the real calamity" in Nietzsche's life (*EH*, 241). Cultivating individuality includes learning what is best for us—our preferences, needs, limitations, capacities, and possibilities.

Nietzsche expected that many of his readers would become impatient with such tangents from intellectual discussion, with such indulgence in matters so personal and seemingly trivial. His reply: "[T]hese small things—nutrition, place, climate, recreation, the whole casuistry of selfishness—are inconceivably more important than everything one has taken to be important so far. Precisely here one must begin to *relearn*" (*EH*, 256). It is because we have been distracted by so many harmful concepts—"'God,' 'soul,' 'virtue,' 'sin,' 'beyond,' 'truth,' 'eternal life'"—that we have despised "the 'little' things . . . the basic concerns of life itself" (*EH*, 256). Relearning the importance of the supposedly little things in life involves more than reading of their importance. It involves attempts to live them.

Acknowledging the importance of basic concerns of living, and attending to the body, is not always limited to small steps and fine tuning. In one of his more restless moments, Nietzsche explains how Zarathustra saw man as

> an un-form, a material, an ugly stone that needs a sculptor. . . . 'But my fervent will to create impels me ever again toward man; thus is the hammer impelled toward stone. . . . *Now my hammer rages cruelly against its prison.* Pieces of rock rain from the stone . . . O my brothers, what are gods to me now?' (EH, 309)[38]

Not everyone will feel the need or have the strength to hammer away at the stone of themselves. The hope is that individuals not feel compelled, despite their inherited culture or morality, to hammer away at themselves and, conversely, that those wanting to hammer away not be discouraged from doing so.

A jolting, powerful account of individuals who have hammered away at themselves is Loren Cameron's *Body Alchemy: Transsexual Portraits*.[39] Through photographs and essays, Cameron recounts her/his journey and those of others through gender nonconformity, ridicule, ostracism, isolation, confusion, self-inflicted injury, attempted suicide, and then through changes in wardrobe, lifestyle, sexual activity, and name, and through piercing, tattooing, exercise, steroid use, and surgery. The goal—and provisional outcome—is not conformity to familiar identities such as "male" or "straight." Indeed, many of the individuals present themselves through unstable, hybrid identities, such as "male lesbian." And some, after years of futile searching for their place in the established matrix of gender and sexuality, give up this search and get on with their individual lives. Cameron's mode of presentation exemplifies the use of affective strategies, and the inducement of surprise and discomfort, to upset established concepts and beliefs.

This chapter has covered many matters in an attempt to convey Nietzsche's corporeal turn. His corporeal turn is more fundamental than his linguistic turn and is something that discussions of Nietzsche, and of corporeality and politics, often neglect. In discussing these matters I have been forced, as was Nietzsche, to rely on terms that presuppose the very distinctions I wish to unsettle. Yet using these terms more self-consciously is a step toward the sort of materialism we may now explore. In the next chapter I attend to the seeming paradox of speaking of thinking, variously, as distinct from the body, as both inspired by and in tension with the body, and as itself bodily. Hampshire helps us to clarify this paradox—and to understand why it cannot be entirely eliminated—and to explore its implications for thinking, ethics, and politics.

NOTES

1. Friedrich Nietzsche, *Twilight of the Idols,* trans. R. J. Hollingdale (New York: Penguin Books, 1990). Hereafter cited *TI.*

2. Hannah Arendt, *The Human Condition* (Chicago: University of Chicago Press, 1958), 293. Eric Blondel, though often instructive when discussing Nietzsche's understandings of metaphysics and the body, repeats this interpretation in *Nietzsche: The Body and Culture,* trans. Sean Hand (London: Athlone Press, 1991), 201–38.

3. Discussion of "a new image of thought" appears in Gilles Deleuze, *Nietzsche and Philosophy,* trans. Hugh Tomlinson (New York: Columbia University Press, 1983), 103–10.

4. Nietzsche proclaims, "I mistrust all systematizers and avoid them. The will to system is a lack of integrity" (*TI,* 35). Bernard Williams observes that Nietzsche's texts have been "mined against [theory's] extraction," that each has been "booby-trapped"

against recovering theory from it or assimilating it to theory. But it does not follow, Williams maintains, that when drawing on Nietzsche our philosophy should contain no theory. Bernard Williams, "Nietzsche's Minimalist Moral Psychology," in *Making Sense of Humanity* (Cambridge: Cambridge University Press, 1995), 66. Such an approach seems to have sufficient integrity.

5. In Blondel's formulation, for Nietzsche the body is an "intermediary space" between the chaos of the world and the simplification of the intellect; it is the point of translation. Blondel, *Nietzsche: The Body and Culture*, 207.

6. Friedrich Nietzsche, *The Will to Power*, trans. Walter Kaufmann and R. J. Hollingdale (New York: Vintage Books, 1968), sec. 1067. Hereafter cited *WP.*

7. See, e.g., *WP,* sec. 584, 639; Friedrich Nietzsche, *Thus Spoke Zarathustra: A Book for None and All,* trans. Walter Kaufmann (New York: Penguin Books, 1966), 166, 201 (hereafter cited *TSZ);* and *TI,* 46–47.

8. Friedrich Nietzsche, *Philosophy and Truth: Selections from Nietzsche's Notebooks of the Early 1870's,* ed. and trans. Daniel Breazeale (Atlantic Highlands, N.J.: Humanities Press International, 1979), 45.

9. See also Nietzsche, *Philosophy and Truth,* 83.

10. Friedrich Nietzsche, *On the Genealogy of Morals,* trans. Walter Kaufmann (New York: Vintage Books, 1989), 26. Hereafter cited *GM.*

11. For a slightly different presentation of Nietzsche's ontology and characterization of the body, resembling Taylor's reading, see Daniel R. Ahern, "The Philosophical Physician: Life as Will to Power," in *Nietzsche as Cultural Physician* (University Park: Pennsylvania University Press, 1995), 9–25. "Nietzsche interprets the totality of being as will to power"; consequently, each individual is "a multiplicity of instincts, all of which demand gratification," each seeking domination over the others (11, 17). See also Paul Patton, "Nietzsche and the Body of the Philosopher," in *Cartographies: Post-Structuralism and the Mapping of Bodies,* ed. R. Diprose and R. Ferrel (Sydney: Allen & Unwin, 1991), 43–54, for the claim that Nietzsche understood the body "as composed of a multiplicity of forces" (46).

12. As captured by one commentator, in contrast to Kant, for whom morality is generated from the faculty of reason, which is the same for all humans, and therefore the morality generated is the same, "[f]or Nietzsche, the entire bodily experience is involved in the generation of values, and different bodies will generate different schemes of value." Robert Ackerman, *Nietzsche: A Frenzied Look* (Amherst: University of Massachusetts Press, 1990), 174 n. 8.

13. Nietzsche's emphasis on the corporeality of moral psychology appears again and again. For further examples, see *WP,* secs. 334, 392, 710; *TI,* 40, 49, 62–63; *GM,* 55; *TSZ,* 31.

14. In discussing Aristotle, Bernard Williams similarly concludes that "people's dispositions . . . in a sense . . . are the ultimate supports of ethical value. That has a practical as well as a metaphysical significance. The preservation of ethical value lies in the

reproduction of ethical dispositions." Bernard Williams, *Ethics and the Limits of Philosophy* (Cambridge: Harvard University Press, 1985), 51. However, adhering to his distinction between "the inside" and "the outside" points of view, Williams appears to maintain that from the inside we are unable to evaluate our dispositions, since they partly constitute the self, and from the outside, abstracted from our dispositions, we are unable to evaluate them, or anything else (51, 65–66, 110). Yet if Williams's distinction is loosened and dispositions are seen as entrenched aspects of the self subject nevertheless to challenge from other regions of the self, possibilities are widened for reflection on disposition and value.

15. Michel Foucault, "Nietzsche, Genealogy, History," in *Language, Countermemory, Practice,* ed. Donald Blouchard (Ithaca: Cornell University Press, 1977), 147.

16. The physiology and "intelligence" of gut reactions is increasingly understood. See Sandra Blakeslee, "Complex and Hidden Brain in the Gut Makes Cramps, Butterflies, and Valium," *New York Times,* 22 March 1996, sec. C, 1, 3.

17. André Gide, *The Immoralist,* trans. Richard Howard (New York: Vintage Books, 1996), vii, 60, 109–10. I was drawn to Gide by the excellent discussion in Leo Bersani, *Homos* (Cambridge: Harvard University Press, 1995), 113–29. Similarly, maintaining the fundamental role of intuition in generating ethical theory, against the hope of establishing ethical theory determinatively through reason, Bernard Williams concludes that, even if basic ethical assumptions are embraced, what they might yield "under immense possible differences in bodily constitution, in sentiment, and generally in what Wittgensteinians call 'form of life,' is a baffling question." Williams, *Ethics and the Limits of Philosophy,* 103.

18. In making a strong case for ad hominem argument and criticism, Robert Solomon contends that it "involves a rich conception of the self, as opposed to the minimal, emaciated, and merely 'transcendental' self—'unencumbered' by emotions, desires, personality, or character—presupposed by so many philosophers from Descartes and Kant to John Rawls." Robert C. Solomon, "Nietzsche *ad hominem:* Perspectivism, Personality, and *Ressentiment,*" in *The Cambridge Companion to Nietzsche,* ed. Bernard Magnus and Kathleen Higgins (Cambridge: Cambridge University Press, 1996), 216–17.

19. See Marc Fisher and Sue Ann Pressley, "Crisis of Sexuality Launched Strange Journey," *Washington Post,* 29 March 1997, A1.

20. Nietzsche is most consistent in maintaining that the "soul" is a superfluous construct, "mendaciously invented . . . to ruin the body" (*EH,* 332, see also 302; *TSZ,* 13, 20, 42, 221). Elsewhere, he articulates his ideals for the self in terms of the depth and richness of the soul (*EH,* 305–6; *TSZ,* 208–9). In accounting for his own creativity Nietzsche says "the *body* is inspired; let us keep the 'soul' out of it" (*EH,* 302). Leslie Paul Thiele, *Friedrich Nietzsche and the Politics of the Soul* (Princeton: Princeton University Press, 1990), nevertheless reads Nietzsche (in a discussion that is, overall, quite illuminating) as rooting plurality and inspiration in the soul. Alan White, *Within Niet-*

zsche's Labyrinth (New York: Routledge, 1990), 72–80, argues that Zarathustra comes to "resurrect" what he earlier repudiated as the soul. My disagreement with these readings is largely semantic, as Nietzsche clearly rejects Platonist and Christian beliefs in an immortal soul that survives a mortal body, and when he writes of the soul, he is almost certainly doing so figuratively. Foucault follows Nietzsche in maintaining that the "soul is the effect and instrument of a political anatomy; the soul is the prison of the body." Michel Foucault, *Discipline and Punish,* trans. Alan Sheridan (New York: Vintage Books, 1979), 30.

21. For a similar interpretation, see Keith Ansell-Pearson, *Nietzsche contra Rousseau* (Cambridge: Cambridge University Press, 1991), 134–49.

22. Similarly, elsewhere Nietzsche introduces self-presentation in terms of "art of style": "To communicate a state, an inward tension of pathos, by means of signs . . . that is the meaning of every style; and considering that the multiplicity of inward states is exceptionally large in my case, I have many stylistic possibilities" (*EH,* 265).

23. Nietzsche, *Philosophy and Truth,* 80.

24. As put by Arthur Kleinman and Byron Good, when exploring the complex intersection of corporeality and culture, "There is no blood test for depression." Arthur Kleinman and Byron Good, introduction to *Culture and Depression: Studies in the Anthropology and Cross-Cultural Psychiatry of Affect and Disorder,* ed. Arthur Kleinman and Byron Good (Berkeley and Los Angeles: University of California Press, 1985), 4.

25. This is in contrast to the position Richard Rorty attributes to historicist thinkers, whom he commends for denying "such a thing as the 'deepest level of the self'" and "insist[ing] that socialization . . . goes all the way down." Richard Rorty, *Contingency, Irony, and Solidarity* (Cambridge: Cambridge University Press, 1989), xiii. Such a conception of the self makes it difficult to appreciate the social criticisms put forth by Nietzsche and Foucault, leading Rorty to overlook certain forms of cruelty, even though the prevention of cruelty is presented as his deepest commitment.

26. See Ansell-Pearson, *Nietzsche contra Rousseau,* 144–45. For specific accounts of the formation of reflective subjects and responsible agents through ritual and bodily techniques, see Talal Asad, *Genealogies of Religion: Discipline and Reasons of Power in Christianity and Islam* (Baltimore: Johns Hopkins University Press, 1993), chaps. 1–4.

27. See also *TI,* 66–67, 107.

28. In Franz Kafka, *The Metamorphosis, In the Penal Colony, and Other Stories,* trans. Joachim Neurgroschel (New York: Simon & Schuster, 1993), 198, 205.

29. Paul Connerton, *How Societies Remember* (Cambridge: Cambridge University Press, 1989), 102.

30. Nietzsche's portrait of Socrates is, of course, highly selective.

31. In grouping consciousness, rationality, and language here, I am not using them interchangeably nor claiming that Nietzsche does so (though in places he seems to). Delineating them further in relation to each other exceeds the scope of this chapter. One of Nietzsche's most suggestive treatments of their relation, in which he conflates

language and conscious, thereby seeing individual thinking, feeling, and acting as not entirely subsumed under (shared) language and (collective) consciousness, appears in *The Gay Science*, trans. Walter Kaufmann (New York: Vintage Books, 1974), 297–300.

32. See also *TSZ*, 126–27, 290. This is best contrasted with the rationalism of Jürgen Habermas, in which an "ideal speech situation" is not clouded by affect and in which disembodied locutions are assessed apart from their embodied location. Yet in *actual* speech situations Habermas's tone is revealing, as when he addresses a nonrationalist by angrily insisting—employing rhetorical means not limited to argument—that "a mood is no substitute for arguments." Jürgen Habermas, "The Unity of Reason in the Diversity of its Voices," in *Postmetaphysical Thinking*, trans. William Mark Hohengarten (Cambridge: MIT Press, 1992), 133. Drawing on Habermas, Mark Warren is unconvincing when claiming that Nietzsche presupposed an ideal of *rational* autonomy and argument in opposition to coercion. See Mark Warren, "Nietzsche and Weber: When Does Reason Become Power?" in *The Barbarism of Reason,* ed. A. Horowitz and T. Maley (Toronto: University of Toronto Press, 1994), 68–96. Habermas himself identifies Nietzsche's rejection of the modern ideal of reason in "The Entry into Postmodernity: Nietzsche as a Turning Point," in *The Philosophical Discourse of Modernity,* trans. Frederick Lawrence (Cambridge: MIT Press, 1987), 83–105.

33. In contrast to Nietzsche, as Richard Sennett perspicaciously and effectively notes, recent discussions of the body often limit themselves to a formal, detached style, and they suffer for it. "Evocations of the feeling body—the slight tremor of an anus when licked, the tightness of cold skin, the surge of pain when a nipple ring is yanked—do not figure in much of this discourse, as though the evocation of sensuality might seduce, and so disorient analysis." Richard Sennett, "The Social Body," *Transition* 6, no. 3 (71): 90.

34. Being allowed two paths is little better than being confined to one. Disturbing illustration of this appears in Daniel Goleman, "'Wrong' Sex: A New Definition of Childhood Pain," *New York Times,* 22 March 1994, sec. B, 6–7. The article canvasses expert opinion regarding "gender identity disorder," in which children exhibit behavior inconsistent with their apparent biological gender. Therapy, which is seldom effective if not begun before the age of ten, involves collaboration between therapists, parents, and teachers, as they set reasonable limits to the child's abnormal behavior. The article is careful to distinguish children with abnormal attitudes toward their normal biology from children with abnormal biology.

35. See, e.g., Martha Nussbaum, "Human Functioning and Social Justice: In Defense of Aristotelian Essentialism," *Political Theory* 20, no. 2 (May 1992): 202–46. The above page references are to this article.

36 For a discussion of liberal and neoconservative objections to Nussbaum and other liberal perfectionists, see Albert W. Dzur, "Liberal Perfectionism and Democratic Participation," *Polity* 30, no. 4 (Summer 1998): 667–90. Dzur proposes, unconvinc-

ingly, that deep conflicts over the ends of life might be agreeably resolved through "public dialogue" and "reasoned deliberation."

37. A recent, sustained attempt to develop such an ethic is William E. Connolly's *The Ethos of Pluralization* (Minneapolis: University of Minnesota Press, 1995).

38. This is importantly different from what is otherwise a remarkably similar passage in Thoreau: "Every man is the builder of a temple, called his body, *to the god he worships*, after a style purely his own, nor can he get off by hammering marble instead. We are all sculptors and painters, and our material is our own flesh and blood and bones." Henry David Thoreau, *Walden* (New York: New American Library, 1980), 150, emphasis mine. For Thoreau, somatic sculpting is done for a god, whereas for Nietzsche such work requires first being "lured . . . away from God and gods, [for] what could one create if gods—were there?" (*EH*, 309).

39. Loren Cameron, *Body Alchemy: Transsexual Portraits* (Pittsburgh: Cleis Press, 1996).

4

SELF-CONSCIOUS MATERIALISM

FREEDOM AND THOUGHT IN STUART HAMPSHIRE

A true self-consciousness makes one aware that one is looking at, and responding to, persons and things from a particular place among other persons and things, a place defined by bodily existence, and with a mind that functions, both in perceiving and in guiding action, under the limitations imposed by this embodiment.

—Stuart Hampshire

Given my discussion of Nietzsche and of Taylor's opposition to Foucault, it would seem natural to turn now to Foucault, a disciple of Nietzsche who has powerfully explored subjectivity, freedom, reflection, and ethics with an emphasis on the body. Instead, I turn to Stuart Hampshire, whose thinking parallels that of Foucault and makes the body a central concern, both of which have gone unremarked. Hampshire also draws from the same source as Nietzsche, as his principal influence—Spinoza—is the only thinker Nietzsche regarded as a precursor. Hampshire does not simply complement Foucault but *exceeds* him, as he explores issues that Foucault identified as critical but did not live to treat fully, most notably the relation of symbolic systems, embodied practices, and ethical sensibilities.

Hampshire illuminates the many respects in which an assumption of materialism, with its attention to the body, has radical implications for how we think and live. Moreover, his ethical and political views—a cautious liberal universalism—largely stem from his treatment of the body, and he carefully identifies the problems inherent in such a position. Turning to

Hampshire thus places us at the center of current discussions within liberalism, which he addresses to limited effect and in which the most distinctive elements in his thinking—his emphasis on the body and his sensibility of ambivalence and regret—have the least effect.[1] Hampshire has proven to be a prescient thinker, one whose main ideas were formulated with the expectation of significant advances in the science of humans, advances that are increasingly becoming a reality. For this reason, now is not the time to ignore his thinking.

NATURE AND CONVENTION

Central to Hampshire's thought is a distinction between nature and convention. The distinction is presented as crucial and unavoidable, but also as inherently unstable and problematical:

> The opposition between nature and artificiality, or convention . . . is a distinction that seems to be indispensable, and yet it cannot be made precise. At least it is part of men's nature to have opinions about what their true nature is; but these opinions are in recurring conflict with each other.[2]

"Nature" is given a number of senses and levels of meaning and employed heuristically and phenomenologically. Nature is conceived in opposition to culture, artifice, and convention, referring to that which is in some sense independent of human design and activity. It refers to that which is most stable and fixed and least subject to alteration, whereas convention refers to that which is more easily subject to alteration and innovation. Of course, objects and processes regarded as natural also change, but less as the result of human activity.

Nevertheless, human activity, and artifice and convention, affect nature, requiring that it be successively redefined and relocated. This is most dramatically the case when technological innovations produce hybrids that are an unprecedented blend of nature and culture. When confronted with such hybrids (e.g., large tomatoes, prosthetic limbs, drug-induced relaxation, cloned sheep), we often wonder whether they should be regarded as "natural." For example, the National Bioethics Advisory Commission concluded in 1998 that a hybrid cow-human cell "raised 'concerns about crossing species boundaries and exercising excessive control over nature,'" making the hybrid not only unnatural, but troublingly and disruptively so.[3] In an age of such hybrids and boundary crossings, especially through genetic engineering and biotechnology, the distinction between nature and convention seems more problematical and complicated than ever. And yet we have difficulty dispensing with it.[4]

We often mistakenly identify convention as nature. This occurs when, long after its introduction, convention becomes stable and sedimented, its origin as artifice forgotten. Some conventions are so internalized by those upholding them as to become "second nature" and, even beyond that, come to be viewed as natural and felt as instinctive.[5] And yet, in attempting not to naturalize convention, it is easy to err on the side of viewing nature and all references to it as *mere* convention.[6] In doing so, we fail to appreciate the extent to which nature can be an independent force influencing and pressuring convention, threatening to undermine its security and stability.

Moreover, *human* nature—the capacities most distinguishing us from the rest of nature, namely, language and reflection—lead us, paradoxically, to be *un*natural, to inhibit and repress our natures, to unify and transform them through shared vocabulary and concepts. Indeed, culture, especially moral prohibition, is conceived by Hampshire to be, at base, a *response* to nature, a response that reshapes it and to some extent violates it. Morality changes that which was not easily susceptible to change. Moral prohibitions "are artifices that give human lives some distinctive, peculiar, even arbitrary human shape and pattern. They humanize the natural phases of experience" (*MC*, 95). Without such artifice, human life would remain in a wholly natural state and to us would appear *in*human. It is thus "natural for us to be unnatural, . . . to be involved in repression and conflict: these are the costs of culture" (*MC*, 169).

Becoming an "adult," an individual fit for a particular culture, is, unavoidably, a process of consolidating and modifying inclinations, of adopting restraints and forging them into habits. We are born into a social world, with language and rules ordering and conflicting with our natural inclinations.[7] Hampshire views such inhibition as leading to an expanded inner life of unexpressed feelings, subdued dispositions, and unpursued desires. As such, his account of the inward self developing as opportunities for action were diminished is similar to the accounts given by Nietzsche and Arendt, although he does not see this as a characteristically modern phenomenon.

Echoing Foucault, Hampshire discusses the way in which our "way of life," the entire ensemble of conventions and prohibitions we enter shortly after birth and inhabit until death, is supported by "trained dispositions" and requires a "museum of normalcies" (*MC,* 148). In place of the accounts given by Plato and Aristotle of disposition and character, in which innate dispositions are cultivated through education to form moral character, Hampshire contends that

> there is no set of natural dispositions which is by itself sufficient to form a normal and natural character, and to which children should be introduced. They have to learn our ways, or to learn someone's foreign or archaic ways. . . . Some potentialities of their nature will never be developed, and they will usually know that; and, perhaps more important, they will feel the repression. (*MC,* 148)

Hampshire is thus taking a position irreducible to two familiar positions. His position is distinct from the Platonist and Aristotelian positions, lurking in Taylor, as it does not presume initial natural disposition to be congruent with eventual moral development.[8] As a result, imposition is seldom avoidable, and numerous paths of development and alternative moral characters are forgone.

Yet neither is his the position, prevalent today, that, in emphasizing the contingency of convention, refuses reference to natural dispositions or inclinations that are, in some sense, *independent of convention* and never fully congruent with it.[9] Instead, Hampshire presumes certain attributes to be, to some extent, independent of convention. He sees convention as contingent but not arbitrarily so, as tethered, if only loosely, to nature. Hampshire offers the analogy of clothing, which, in all of its possibility and variety, bears some relation to the body (*MC,* 152). Clothing suggests the shape of the body lying beneath; it affects the body, accentuating certain dimensions and diminishing others, and is often felt to be a poor fit. Yet this analogy is lacking, as convention and nature are far less easily distinguished than clothing and the body. And convention affects nature more systemically than clothing does the body. Convention is best seen not as a surface phenomenon, concealing nature, but as seeping into and reconstituting nature.

Finally, there is a sense in which nature refers to that which, at present, is most stable and fixed. As such, freedom, like convention, is defined in opposition to nature and is given two senses. In the first sense, freedom involves identifying nature—again, that which is most stable and fixed— and making choices and acting in the domain of convention, of the unstable and the unfixed. In the second, rarer and more radical sense, freedom involves challenging and *upsetting* that which is stable and fixed. In this sense, freedom involves an intervention into nature, unsettling and reconfiguring the distinction between nature and culture, denaturalizing that which was viewed as natural, unfixing that which was presumed to be fixed.[10]

In contrast, Taylor sees freedom, fundamentally, as not challenging, upsetting, or altering nature but as achieving *attunement* with it. Many contemporary thinkers concerned with ecology, the growth of technology, and the domination of nature share Taylor's emphasis on attunement, respect, and harmony in human-nature interactions. Such thinkers would no doubt find Hampshire's position to be a recipe for disaster, as it encourages us to upset the balance between humans and nature. These worries are not without warrant, but as presented they naturalize nature in a way that limits human options. The thinkers might sensibly respond that not limiting options produces the horrible consequences we see today. But viewing such limited options as enhanced freedom is dubious.

All of us are born into both a natural and a conventional order. In the above senses of freedom, maturity involves distinguishing these orders and, occasionally and more radically, contesting and upsetting them.[11] Distinguishing nature from convention is not, of course, a single event. Nor is the distinction always universal. Rather, it is more often local and relative to us, as we distinguish what can be altered from what cannot be. We assess our surroundings and our bodily state, gathering information and making judgments as to what is fixed and what is possible in a particular situation. And we imagine how the range of possibilities might be enlarged, how our present purposes and intentions might be revised and new ones formed.[12] The agent

> must find the various paths of practical possibility in the situation before him . . .
> He has nothing to decide . . . in respect of those things that are certain to happen
> in the natural course of events [or] in respect of those things which it is not in his
> power to change, because he has not the means, or the opportunity, or the author-
> ity, or the skill. The agent necessarily sees a contrast between the fixed elements in
> the situation and the elements changeable by him. . . . The range of his own
> thoughts and interests will determine, within the limits of the changeable, as he
> sees it, the narrower possibilities of action between which he chooses. (*FI*, 82–83)

So things are occurring, and we are thinking and acting, on a number of levels. We are assessing our situation, including our bodily state, to determine what can be altered and what cannot be, and to anticipate what our situation and our bodily state may become. We are attempting to better understand how our situation and our bodily state affect our thoughts, intentions, purposes, and desires and may be unnecessarily foreclosing possibilities. We are struggling to identify how our thoughts, intentions, purposes, and desires may limit our possibilities further, beyond the limits set by the situation itself or by our bodily state. And we are searching for means that allow us to alter our situation and our bodily state—allowing new thoughts, intentions, purposes, and desires and thus a new configuration of possibilities.[13] In such complex, *layered* situations we identify and modify nature and convention, with each domain affecting the other and the multiple layers modifying one another.

Hampshire's views on nature and convention are elucidated in his discussion of Marquis de Sade, whom he reads as providing a general theory of nature and of human nature. Sade's two starting points are summarized as, first, the claim that there is nothing outside or higher than the order of nature and, second, that our behavior results from our nature, our physical makeup and organization.[14] Consequently, Sade looked forward to advances in the science of anatomy that would allow humans to understand, and thereby to respect and better accommodate, the urges moving them, a science eclipsing the study of law and morality. Such a thorough-going determinism would seem to lead to a simple, mechanistic view of things, but it need not. Instead, Sade emphasized the intricacy of individual makeup, urging each individual to "realiz[e] experimentally all the contradictory impulses that Nature had implanted in him," to uncover his own secret, morally concealed operations (S, 58).

This distinguished Sade from other Enlightenment thinkers, who also "believed that freedom depended on living in accordance with nature, truthfully discovered." Sade differed both in his *method* of discovery and in his conclusions. Whereas Hume and others were content with general classifications of human motive, gleaned from accounts of overt behavior, Sade sought to go *beneath* general classifications and behaviors, to explore the darkest, deepest recesses of each individual, to uncover the "great range of distinct impulses and emotions, peculiar to human beings and unrelated to a single biological need" (S, 57–58).

Such probing led Sade to conclusions beyond those of his contemporaries. He concluded that *sexual* impulses and emotions are the foundation of individual temperament and character; that human desires are polymorphous and therefore "that socially recognized normality is only one specialization" of desire among other possibilities; and that primary impulses are ambivalent, entailing that apparently pure emotions are artificial, precarious organizations of them (S, 59). Artifice and organization are for this reason never wholly secure, as contradictory and muted impulses, unsatisfied desires, and smothered feelings are not extinguished. Rather, they remain as pressures, threatening to undermine settled, unifying artifice, to overwhelm civilized restraints.

For Sade, "to live as one should live is to live in accord with one's original Nature, and in an awakened enjoyment of its possibilities" (S, 59–60). To do so is not necessarily to achieve a state of harmony, in which individuals are liberated and in accord with natural impulse, but often one of heightened conflict, as dissonant elements are unleashed. This is why Sade was not surprised that the French Revolution, in its lifting of restraints, had the double face of both liberation and terror. Unlike the consoling naturalism of Sade's contemporaries, his commends "probing after intimate self-knowledge" as we "listen to, and analyze, the movements of our imagination and of our desires, provided that we are not too frightened by that which we dimly suspect we may find there" (S, 60–61). The outcome of such "solitary experiment[s] in self-knowledge" is not to change our make-up or to sedate our impulses and imaginings but to know them better, to appreciate their subtle differences from those of other individuals, to live with them and attempt to set them free in action and words (S, 61).

These issues are explored in Peter Weiss's fascinating play *The Persecution and Assassination of Jean-Paul Marat as Performed by the Inmates of the Asylum of Charenton under the Direction of the Marquis de Sade.*[15] (Sade did in fact stage elaborate plays with other inmates while imprisoned.) The character Sade says to the revolutionary leader Marat:

> as I sat there in the Bastille
> for thirteen long years
> I learned
> that this is a world of bodies
> each pulsing with a terrible power
> each body alone and racked with its own unrest
> …
> these cells of the inner self
> are worse than the deepest stone dungeon
> and as long as they are locked
> all your revolution remains
> only a prison mutiny
> to be put down
> by corrupted fellow-prisoners. (92–93)

In reviewing a performance of this play, Hampshire notes that when liberating pulsing bodies, even Sade knew that it was easy to get hurt, and so often he limited himself, ironically, to the realm of "theatrical artifice."[16]

Sade's is not, needless to say, a formula for restraint. Hampshire does not endorse Sade's "casual brutality" and "life of absolute license" (S, 61, 62), as it makes choices, such as valuing freedom to the exclusion of all else, that Hampshire does not make. Along with Nietzsche, Sade understates the commonality and stability of certain human needs and aspirations that may provide a basis for a minimal, shared morality, setting acceptable limits to transgression. But Sade's characterization of nature, human nature, and morality—their tensions and entanglement—is instructive. We may join

Hampshire (and Sade) in not becoming wholly Sadean, while cultivating a sensibility that is *haunted by Sade*.[17]

EXPLANATION AND FREEDOM

Even more central to Hampshire's thinking, underlying his discussion of nature and convention, and explanation and freedom, is a commitment to materialism—to "*self-conscious* materialism"—as a conception of being and doctrine of personality.[18] Hampshire's materialism allows him to conceive explanation and freedom not as opposed but as complementary. Others conceive them as opposed, contrasting the realm of material causation categorically with that of human choice and freedom and seeing the powers of thought as transcending the natural order. Yet explanation and freedom can complement one another, because explaining one's thought and action is itself an act of freedom, serving to augment and reconfigure one's freedom.

Hampshire's position is distinct from what he identifies as the two prevalent alternatives. It is distinct from extra-materialism, which avoids seeing humans in wholly material terms or reducing them to one kind of material object among others, as this is seen as diminishing—indeed, eliminating—choice and freedom (KM, 211–12). It is also distinct from "crass materialis[m]," which does not consider sufficiently the implications of materialism for the *thinking* human and which does not appreciate the "inexhaustibility of description," in which being exceeds any account of it.[19] Surpassing these positions, Hampshire elaborates "self-conscious materialism," which strives to be consistent in its materialism, not conceiving freedom as occurring on a plane above that of physical causation or as eluding explanation. Rather, it emphasizes the extent to which our descriptions of, and reflections on, the material realm itself modify this realm. Hampshire thus urges a "Copernican revolution" in the study of humans, in order to grasp sufficiently "the complex physical processes in which our thought is embodied" (KM, 222). He anticipates increasingly successful applications of science to the study of thinking and personality.

The self-conscious materialist does not ask whether certain activity *really* requires a physical or psychological explanation, as if it must be, ultimately, one or the other.[20] For example, if the mechanisms of thought are damaged, thought is impaired; if a thought is suggested to the mind, bodily mechanisms are equivalently affected (KM, 231).[21] All of us, at some level, know this. Yet "[o]ur language is still so thoroughly dualistic and Cartesian that it is very difficult to grasp, and to hold on to, [this] alternative model" (KM, 231). Our reflections and interventions largely retain this dualism, even as we struggle to unsettle and transcend it.

The complexity and subtlety of Hampshire's materialism stems from his emphasis on *the power of thought*. He begins by assuming that the human capacity for thought must be studied as are other abilities and activities, as embodied in physical mechanisms and processes, presumed to be immensely complex (KM, 211). Including the power of thought as a physical phenomenon, which can be made the object of explanation, is in contrast to the position maintaining that, by its very nature, thought cannot be made the object of psychophysical explanation (KM, 212–13). Although there is no limit, in principle, to explanation, it cannot be definitive and seldom is it sufficient. This is due to the inexhaustibility of description and to the fact that explanation is an exercise of thought that, once offered, calls for explanation. Explanation of this exercise is at once illuminating and insufficient, as it alters the phenomenon, thereby calling for further explanation.

Crass materialists, who share Hampshire's assumption of the possibility of unlimited psychophysical explanation, do not, however, pursue the *practical* implications of their thesis. As a result, they avoid questions that for any individual are unavoidable:

> Suppose that a man is once convinced that all the distinct operations of his mind are embodied in distinct bodily processes, . . . [S]uppose also that he already has some of the required knowledge of the physical embodiments of his own thought: how will he then interpret and evaluate, in light of this detailed knowledge, his own thoughts and sentiments, together with the conduct that expresses them? Materialists have not persistently asked themselves what it would be like actually to *be* a materialist, living and acting with some specific knowledge that a materialist claims must be obtainable. What would it be like to apply this exact

knowledge, once obtained, to oneself, every day, in forming one's own attitudes, sentiments, and purposes? (KM, 213)

This is a remarkable passage, as it challenges us—especially us, as we live in an age in which knowledge of the psychophysical mechanisms of thought is advancing and in which the ability to influence these mechanisms, especially through medication, is considerable—to incorporate this thesis into our conceptions of selfhood, personality, and thinking and into our daily living. Many of us *already* incorporate self-conscious materialism into our daily lives, but we join philosophers in being far less likely to incorporate it into our conceptions.[22]

The crass materialist thus omits himself from his portrait of the mind-body relation, overlooking his use of knowledge of his situation, and of his bodily state and capacities, in exploring the world. In contrast, the self-conscious materialist emphasizes that, "as an observer of a world of objects, which includes himself, he has to make allowances for his own physical situation and bodily state and dispositions, and for the particular standpoint from which he happens to be observing the world" (KM, 214). In making these allowances, he relies on knowledge of his body in order to reflect on his thinking, and he recognizes that his reflection is itself bodily activity, arising from and in turn affecting his body.

The self-conscious materialist also induces changes in her body in order to notice the effects on her perceptions and thinking (KM, 215). Her body is for her "the instrument that registers effects," it is the "physical equipment" upon which she relies in her transactions with the world, in forming and revising beliefs and sentiments. And it is the object upon which she reflects, her reflections themselves bodily activity, subject to further stages of reflection (KM, 215). She realizes not only that her body limits her transactions with the world, determining levels of accessibility, but also that she may better identify the limited capacities of her body and in doing so may compensate for or extend its limits. The self-conscious materialist makes "thoughtful allowances for [her] particular standpoint," reflecting on her instrument and mechanisms of thought and, in doing so, modifying them and consequently modifying her thought (KM, 216). As the mechanisms of thought are increasingly understood, she makes further modifications in her thinking and achieves new levels in her reflection.

In practice, most of us are, to a considerable extent, self-conscious materialists. We have at least tacit knowledge of our bodies and rely on this knowledge when thinking, and when reflecting on and evaluating our thinking, such as when we dissociate ourselves from a sentiment that we attribute to a particular bodily state. For example, I might realize that my anger toward a particular individual stems largely from my present irritableness, itself the result of my recent cessation of smoking, and upon realizing this reevaluate my anger and, in the hope of overcoming it, take tactical steps to alleviate my irritableness (nicotine patches, one last cigarette). In such cases, my thinking suggests tactics to apply to myself, and these tactics in turn affect the tonalities, intensities, and direction of my thinking.

Given the possibilities for increasing knowledge of the instrument and mechanisms of thought, the self-conscious materialist is interested in technologies for modifying and improving thought, much as technology has modified and improved vision (KM, 219). Such advances in knowledge, far from simplifying or deflating thought, add complexity and depth to it. Previously unavailable knowledge of the body allows individuals to reinterpret their psychophysical states, relying on this knowledge to evaluate, guide, and advance their thinking. New thinking is again subjected to such interpretation. In doing so we better evaluate and more carefully modify thought and are often led to new thoughts. Each stage of reflection, embodied as it is in mechanisms of thought, can itself be reflected upon and rethought. This "reflexive" or "feed-back" process continues indefinitely, adding layer upon layer of complexity to thought and action (KM, 216). Accounts of the physical processes involved in our thinking are not *substitutes* for thinking but rather are *stages* in thinking, not reductions but rather augmentations and added dimensions.

Hampshire anticipates (again, presciently) advances in knowledge of the instrument and mechanisms of thought and subsequent revision of conceptions of selfhood, personality, and thinking, amounting to "a radical and difficult conversion in men's inner life" (KM, 221). The difficulty of this conversion is due in part to the challenge of gaining remove from one's strongest, deepest passions and sentiments. To reflect on your present anger as a psychophysical phenomenon, not wholly warranted by the object to which it refers, but rather arising largely as a result of your bodily state and dispositions, is made difficult by the very strength of your anger. Your passions and sentiments themselves, once they have arisen, can reinforce and prolong ignorance of your bodily state, compelling you to focus on their object (the person who, you feel, *really does* deserve scorn). In such situations you are less likely to consider how your feelings arose.

A self-conscious materialist, however, must strive for this detachment, if she seriously believes what she claims to believe (KM, 222–23). She cannot maintain naive assumptions about the relation of her sentiments to their objects or fail to scrutinize particular sentiments once she has recognized the complexity and the contingency of the psychophysical factors involved in her sentiments (KM, 223). The implications of self-conscious materialism are evident in the testimony of formerly severely depressed individuals whose moods have been elevated by antidepressant medication. Many feel as if their personalities changed radically, as the values, sentiments, habits, appetites, lifestyle, and relationships characterizing their earlier depressed state are no longer fitting and must be replaced or significantly modified.[23]

Reflecting on the factors giving rise to a sentiment sometimes relieves us of it, and accounts of our subsequent psychophysical states must then refer to our reflections on our initial state (KM, 224). For this reason, knowledge of the bodily changes associated with changes in sentiments and attitudes continuously complicates our initial accounts of sentiments and attitudes, modifying them and suggesting possibilities for inducing new ones. You may not wish to have certain sentiments and attitudes, having concluded that they are in some manner unwarranted or undesirable, and may attempt to alter your bodily state in order to alter the sentiment or attitude. Sedative medication, for example, may allow you to achieve a state of relaxation that alleviates what you concluded to be unwarranted stress and worry and may provide the calm needed to reflect further on the origins of your stresses and worries. Or you may, periodically, experiment in your interventions, altering your bodily state, such as through a stimulating drug or invigorating activity, to see what new sentiments and attitudes are enabled. New thinking gives rise again to this sequence, taking you in directions you could not have anticipated.

Hampshire limits his discussions by emphasizing reliable interventions more than experimental ones, directed toward previously defined goals rather than those not yet defined. And he leans toward wanting two separate, independent accounts of thinking, one referring to the rational association of ideas and the other to bodily processes. Similarly, he distinguishes the *reason* for a sentiment from the *explanation* for it, seeing the former as appropriately influenced by arguments and the latter by techniques (*FI*, 86). These categorical separations then emerge in his discussions of morality and politics, in which rational deliberation is contrasted with passionate conflict. As Taylor and Nietzsche convey, we may more subtly maintain that the "rational" association of ideas often involves less rational thinking and others aspects of bodily activity.

Yet it is easy to follow Hampshire in discussing these matters in terms that are too dualistic and categorical, too causal and mechanistic. It is better to maintain, as in places he does, the much cloudier position that every change in thought is also a change in the body, that mental and bodily processes are "each reflections of the other, with neither of them privileged as substance to shadow" (KM, 226). Doing so emphasizes the multiple ways in which thinking and the body can be conceived, described, and experienced and highlights both the effects and the insufficiency of particular conceptions, descriptions, and experiences. This itself loosens the hold of any particular vocabulary for discussing these matters.

The above discussions—of the unstable distinction between nature and convention, of how self-knowledge includes knowledge of one's body, of the ways in which altering one's body can affect one's thinking, and of the power of reflection—allude to underemphasized dimensions of the *experience* of freedom. I can now elaborate these allusions.[24]

I have emphasized the *levels* and *layers* of thinking, as our thoughts are continually checked and modified by second- and third-order thoughts, giving us "thoughts about thoughts, and so on indefinitely" (KM, 227). Our power of reflection allows us to avoid passivity and complacency with regard to thoughts and feelings and their accompanying bodily states. The materialist thesis need not entail, as it does for the crass materialist, that we see ourselves as unfree, or even as less free, upon accounting for the physical bases of thought. Rather, such accounts may make us more free, even *differently* and *unprecedentedly* free, as we identify that which is subject to alteration and, following attempts to alter it, induce changes in our thinking and feeling.[25] Indeed, we may become more effective in achieving our objectives, as we are less subject to causes beyond our purview. In this respect, there is a more complex relation between explanation and freedom than is typically assumed, a relationship that is not, *pace* Arendt, best conceived as antithetical. Nor is the portrait of freedom as situated and layered reducible to a distinction between negative and positive freedom, as formulated by Taylor.[26]

Moreover, this portrait is in contrast to a familiar position, upheld by Arendt and Taylor, and at times by Nietzsche, that sees advances in science as encroaching upon or domesticating human freedom. Rather, scientific advances often augment and reconfigure freedom. The ability to explain that of which we were previously ignorant, or grasped only dimly, can open up new possibilities. It can allow us to intervene in our situation, including our bodily state, so as to enlarge our capacities and to focus on that which is subject to alteration. In doing so we appreciate our *relative* freedom, in which we think and act within certain bounds, better grasping and sometimes reconfiguring these bounds.

We are not, then, best described as "imprisoned" by the bounds of our thought and established interests (*TA*, 184–85). A prison is, in essence, rigid containment from which no amount of effort allows escape. Yet even if the limitations of our thoughts and interests result largely from causes outside our control and beyond our understanding, we retain a degree of freedom. We can explore new thoughts and modify our interests, and then work tactically upon ourselves to move our feelings closer to our thoughts. Our power of reflection—our ability to gain distance from certain thoughts and sentiments, to describe ourselves differently, to identify the factors influencing our conduct, and even to explain the causes of our thoughts— gives us the power to transform our thoughts and interests. Identifying our limitations, bringing them to consciousness, and assessing their degree of fixity itself helps to modify these limitations. Our world of thoughts and interests is, at any moment, bounded and limited, but not as a prison yard. It is far more porous and elastic.

Hampshire suggests that it is our *responsibility* not to acquiesce immediately to natural and social limits but to seek ways to overcome them (*TA*, 186–87). This echoes Foucault's ideal for critical thought:

> [I]t will separate out, from the contingency that has made us what we are, the possibility of no longer being, doing, or thinking what we are, do or think. . . . [I]t is seeking to give new impetus, as far and wide as possible, to the undefined work of freedom. . . . I shall thus characterize the philosophical ethos appropriate to the critical ontology of ourselves as a historico-practical test of the limits we may go beyond, and thus as work carried out by ourselves upon ourselves as free beings.[27]

The above paragraphs are offered as an interpretation of such "undefined work of freedom."

Instances of identifying our limits, what is fixed in our situation and what is open, and of exploiting these openings or creating new ones, are crucial *moments* of freedom in which clarity is achieved and possibilities are glimpsed, and *occasions* of transcendence in which we are relieved of familiar expectations and restraints (*MC*, 57–58). They are a liberal, individualist complement to Arendt's portrait of republican freedom as momentary, short-lived, and extraordinary.

As I shall discuss later, such moments and occasions of freedom are a principal reason for the inadequacy of any comprehensive morality. Comprehensive moralities are limited and limiting, as they cannot anticipate or accommodate "leaps of the imagination, moments of insight, . . . which will lead to transformations of experience and to new moral ambitions and to new enjoyments of living" (*MC*, 125). Comprehensive moralities cannot, by their very nature, make room for advances in knowledge and in human possibility that exceed them. They can neither anticipate advances nor evaluate them, in advance, as a moral *advance*. For this reason, any morality that truly values freedom must not see itself as comprehensive. It must, rather, have a looser, more tentative and porous quality, and must not offer a framework that claims to cover all events and emergences.

Parts of this section may appear to exceed the limits of political theory. Yet these issues in metaphysics and philosophy of mind bear on fundamental questions in political theory, especially regarding political reflection.

They have crucial connections that are too often overlooked. In the remaining sections I flesh out these connections.

REFLECTION AND DECISION

In elaborating Hampshire's conceptions of explanation and freedom, I have, necessarily, begun to elaborate a conception of reflection. The topics must be discussed in conjunction, since freedom resides, not entirely but crucially, in reflection. As I have begun to describe, Hampshire emphasizes the respects in which reflection involves "stepping back" from our situation—including aspects of our bodily situation—and in doing so altering it. Reflection is *spiral*, as our reflection results in a new situation that itself can be stepped back from and reflected upon, and *layered*, as we have reflections upon reflections upon reflections, each modifying those beneath it and sustaining those above it. Each stage of reflection is bodily activity and, viewed as bodily activity, calls for another stage of reflection. Reflection involves experimentation and intervention, as we alter our bodily situation, in part through the very act of reflection, and await the outcome. The outcome may be an unfamiliar feeling, mood, or thought, calling for additional reflection and further experiments and interventions.

Now I elaborate Hampshire's conception of reflection in three respects: first, in which reflection involves considering one's body as it contributes to and limits perspective and thinking; second, in which it involves identifying one's feelings, sentiments, and dispositions; and, third, in which it involves consolidating them through decision. The first, embodiment as contributing to and limiting perspective and thinking, is presented as fundamental to epistemology and ethics, to thinking and thoughtfulness. Self-consciousness involves an appreciation that one is "looking at, and responding to, persons and things from a particular place among other persons and things, a place defined by bodily existence, and with a mind that functions, both in perceiving and in guiding action, under the limitations imposed by this embodiment" (*MC*, 62). Assessing one's overall situation—identifying limits, distinguishing that which is alterable from that which is not, and anticipating changes—includes assessing one's bodily situation.

Such assessments and, subsequently, enhanced abilities deepen thinking. Such deepening may widen one's field of choices and suggest new possibilities for action (*FI*, 81–83).

Bound up with our efforts to assess and modify our bodily situation are our efforts to identify—to clarify and sometimes to wholly discover— obscure feelings, desires, and sentiments. We sometimes painfully identify and discover desires that we had previously excluded, that were unknown to us or antithetical to the desires we professed. Through "various techniques of introspection" we learn of the inchoate and often contradictory or confused desires and inclinations within us, and probe beneath those that are apparent to explore those that may lie beneath. Moreover, often we are led to conceal from others and from ourselves the complexity and contradictoriness of our desires (*FI*, 45). This predicament—that the complexity and contradictoriness of our desires and inclinations require us to simplify and unify them—leads to the topics of sincerity and decision.

Hampshire begins his essay "Sincerity and Single-Mindedness" with the claims that "sincerity is a dubious, uncertain ideal, and . . . it is very difficult to attain. It is not something obvious and simple, and it is not true that we all know what it is."[28] This is not, needless to say, what most of us were taught. Sincerity, in the ordinary view, consists of correspondence between our inner and outer selves, between our thoughts and feelings and our speech and action, whereas insincerity consists of disjunction between the former and the latter. In its ideal form, sincerity requires singleness or undividedness of mind, congruity between inner states and outer expressions (SSM, 245). Such congruity is often difficult to achieve, as it requires that we inventory our thoughts and feelings and, further, that we align them with one another and, further still, that we clarify them so that they can be expressed adequately in speech and action. Thorough inventory of thoughts and feelings requires "self-watching," vigilantly searching for that lurking in hidden recesses of the self, in order to be sure that we have missed nothing (SSM, 233, 248).[29]

Aligning our thoughts and feelings—as expression can only be sincere if certain thoughts and feelings fully occupy us—requires us to select those with which we wish to identify, those that seem genuinely "ours" (SSM,

241). Upon identifying the sentiments to be selected as ours, we must accentuate them, often displacing or denying, suppressing or smothering, contrary sentiments. These two steps—identifying our sentiments and making some of them *genuinely* ours—are reflection and decision.

It is in order to clarify one's sentiments, to identify them in their variety and complexity, to distinguish those acquired from those seemingly natural, and to specify their causal relation to external circumstances that "one is driven to reflection" (SSM, 247). Moreover, since often our habituation is incomplete, and our morality fails to seal us off from alternative assessments of our sentiments and dispositions, identification of radical conflict within us amounts to "subversive reflection" (*MC,* 149). It is subversive in that it unsettles our settled habits and morality, it acknowledges subordinate, latent, or repressed dispositions and inclinations.

Any moral agent with an enduring character, stable dispositions, and reliable conduct, with priorities and values, commitments and attachments, must rid herself of certain feelings and inclinations. She must accentuate some and extinguish others. To do so, often she must rely on *techniques* for ridding herself of feelings that are painful or harmful, that give rise to unwanted thoughts and sentiments.[30] Techniques may be other than arguments, analyses, and the like. Indeed, it is often *after* one is convinced of particular beliefs that one targets the feelings that were bound up with and sustained one's earlier, since-repudiated beliefs (*FI,* 40, 84–86, 99–100). At this point, attempts to alter our beliefs consist less of convincing ourselves of them (for we have already done this) than of searching for effective techniques for altering aspects of ourselves at odds with them. We may find that, even though our beliefs have changed, we are powerless to alter or to control remaining, dissonant aspects of ourselves (*FI,* 105).

Consider, for example, a white adult raised in the American South who has changed her mind on a number of issues regarding racial relations. Following study and discussion, she has come to reject the view that, though it ought not be sanctioned by law, racial separation is preferable to integration. Far more than her grandparents and considerably more than her parents, she is comfortable around blacks, as she has a number of black coworkers, and she has voted for black political candidates and admired black athletes. She finds, however, that when she encounters an interracial couple, especially when one of the persons is unusually dark-skinned and the other unusually light, her stomach turns. And when the couple involves a black man and a white woman, she especially despises the man and worries about the woman. She is ashamed of such repeated reactions, as they are not in accord with beliefs that she feels committed to and wants to profess, but rather unsettle these beliefs. She reassesses her beliefs and concludes, once again, that she is intellectually committed to racial equality. And she reconsiders her ideals, concluding once again that she hopes for a pluralistic, integrated society. Yet her stomach still turns.

Any number of techniques might be adopted to lessen her feelings of revulsion. She might work with a therapist to identify early experiences that led to these feelings, probing her own sexual feelings toward blacks and her attitudes toward sex. Or she might seek to acclimate herself to interracial relations by spending time in mixed settings, gradually relaxing and interacting more with others. Or she might develop an appreciation for art that portrays interracial relations, exposing herself to the perceptions of those who find beauty in such chromatic juxtaposition.

This is not to say that such extensive and intimate work on oneself should be obligatory in a polity, that all of one's deepest, most hidden desires and impulses need to be aligned with one's professed commitments and public actions. To say so would be to uphold the worst in thinkers such as Augustine and Rousseau, which Arendt warns us against and which Taylor leans toward doing. Instead, the woman in the above example might choose to practice nondiscrimination in public settings but avoid interracial couples in her personal life, maintaining a demeanor of respect while submerging her lingering revulsion. But when such compartmentalizing fails, as it often does, we need to engage in multifaceted reflection, probing and assessing our contradictory thoughts and feelings, deciding which parts of ourselves we admire and which we dislike, which we will go with and which we will kill off.[31]

To discuss only the voluntary employment of such techniques would be naive, as there appears to be increasing willingness on the part of authorities to mandate their use. Consider recent attempts in Portland, Oregon, to rehabilitate approximately 950 sex offenders (referred to by a social worker as "scum" who "deserve to be miserable," and including adolescents who had sex with siblings a year younger than they) in a program of "community-based corrections." It is community based, because authorities are confident that offenders, instead of being incarcerated, can be corrected while remaining under surveillance in the community. The program centers on "cognitive restructuring," achieved through techniques such as attaching sensors to the subjects' bodies (monitoring heart rate, blood pressure, salivation, and erection), having them listen to an account of their sexual crime and, upon display of arousal, exposing them immediately to nauseating substances (including ammonia, rotten eggs, spoiled meat covered with maggots, and feces). The goal is to make subjects repulsed by their desires. The program also includes, for men, medication that greatly lowers testosterone levels, leading not only to impotence but also to significant changes in physique and appearance. A supervising psychologist expresses impatience with the subjects' inability, and even more with their refusal, to dispense with certain desires and "errors in thinking."[32]

This need to kill off aspects of oneself amounts to a *decisionism*. Each of us must distinguish, Hampshire maintains, between that which we *discover* about ourselves—about our sentiments, feelings, impulses, and desires—and that which, stepping back from these discoveries, we *decide* about ourselves (*FI*, 104). Such decisions do not simply report our feelings but rather shape and consolidate them. The moral formation of oneself—attempting to achieve a coherent identity and stable character and, in order to do so, relying on techniques to variously accentuate and subordinate aspects of oneself—is captured as follows:

> A man may on reflection want to be the kind of man who has certain interests and desires; he may cultivate certain interests in himself, and may try to smother or to divert others, in pursuit of some ideal of character. This reflexiveness—the desire not to have certain desires—is unavoidable in anyone who reflects and criticizes. (*FI*, 93)

Such decisions are always, in part, *negations*. Most of us feel divisions and conflicts within, and in choosing between contrasting sets of values and ways of life, each of which has its pull on us, and in making a definite, often irreversible choice between them, we feel as if we have repressed or killed part of ourselves. Decisionism on an individual level is importantly analogous to that expounded by Carl Schmitt, for whom the body politic and group identity require such negations and exclusions. For Schmitt, conflicts need to be aired and then, following a decision, need to be muted in order to achieve unity and stability. For both thinkers, decisions *clarify* and are thus decisive. Such decisions are to some extent arbitrary, as they are *under*determined by reason, ideals, or principles but rather involve commitment, a bold leap, and (for Schmitt) unflinching conviction.[33] We must accept responsibility for such choices and commitments, as they are *ours*, authored by us and thus made authoritative, even though not determined by reason or supported by external authority (*MC,* 42).

Indeed, freedom entails such negation. It is only by having a plurality of possibilities from which to choose, as we decide on a way of life, that we can be said to be self-directed and free (*MC,* 32, 93). But exercising choice—the moment of freedom—entails a subsequent unfreedom, a negation of possibilities. "A decision in an ultimate conflict may commit [an] agent to a way of life which will extend in time indefinitely, . . . it will close certain possibilities to him forever, even though they are possibilities that he had thought of as being very highly desirable and valuable" (*MC,* 120). Hampshire continues this point, seizing on the same historical example as does Foucault:

> [T]he ideal of friendship between young males in some ancient Greek cities is thought to have entailed a cost in the ideal of romantic love between men and women, and perhaps also in the ideal of married love, ideals that have prevailed in other places and at other times. Individuals inevitably become conscious of the cost exacted by their own way of life and of the other possibilities of achievement and enjoyment discarded. They feel the cost in internal conflict also. Every established way of life has its cost in repression. (*MC,* 146–47)

Such foreclosed possibilities and lost opportunities, such self-imposed limitation and deliberate impairment, are essential to identity and character, freedom, and morality.

This is a pessimistic conception of the ethics and politics of the self. It is a conception in which forfeiture and forgetting are required, in which we feel and regret limitations and losses, in which we remain ambivalent and unsatisfied, in which we see ourselves "going lop-sided to the grave"

(*MC*, 158). It is an unusually modest conception, one in which we strive not for complete satisfaction with our life choices but merely for a way of life of which we are not ashamed and do not despise or too strongly regret.

Hampshire's conception is a needed antidote to Taylor's more optimistic conception (not to mention the far more optimistic and less nuanced popular conceptions), in which we may achieve satisfaction and in which divisions and tensions within oneself are essentially overcome. But Hampshire's conception is *too* pessimistic and modest. It understates the extent to which individuals can seek cultures or subcultures that are more accommodating and less injurious, and the extent to which political action can seek to establish and maintain such cultures and subcultures. It understates the extent to which tensions can be carefully maintained and past decisions can be undone, instead of eliminating divisions and killing off aspects of ourselves once and for all. And it understates the extent to which identity can remain more fluid by harboring tension and juggling multiple, alternative self-understandings, and the extent to which a pluralistic, fluid culture can facilitate this. Nevertheless, Hampshire is correct that even the most fluid, open, accommodating culture involves regrettable negations and foreclosures, both socially and individually.

MORALITY AND CONFLICT

Morality sets itself a difficult task. It is rooted in the very conflicts it seeks to resolve, appealing to that which is natural, normal, necessary, right, desirable, or agreeable in precisely those areas in which these are disputed. Morality is a response to conflict that risks spawning greater conflict. Morality often involves distinguishing nature from mere convention, that which is universal and permanent from that which is merely local and provisional, and those matters on which we expect convergence from those on which we allow divergence. Hampshire's treatment of morality stems from his views discussed above, as he attempts, cautiously, to identify stable and constant human needs beneath varying and fluctuating desires, to uncover minimal commonalities beneath substantial differences. Far more than most universalists, Hampshire emphasizes how difficult it is to arrive at a universal morality and how limited the scope of such a morality must be.

Nevertheless, the most creative moments and promising themes in Hampshire's thinking are often subdued in his discussions of morality. His commitment to immanent materialism in place of transcendental idealism, and his explorations of an ethic of life in place of a morality of law, are eclipsed by a cold, formal proceduralism, a "machinery of arbitration."[34] Proceduralism is believed to be necessary to protect life from the destructive, antilife impulses unleashed by an ethic of life. Hampshire fears that an ethic of life, with its privileging of the body, may lead to celebration of strength, uncompromising individualism, and eventually license and cruelty.

This fear leads to his eventual rejection of Sade and to his quicker rejection of Nietzsche. Indeed, Hampshire begins *Morality and Conflict* by contrasting the philosophical tradition (from Plato to Rawls) with Nietzsche, contending that although its claims for reason and harmony are overstated, the tradition is of value despite Nietzsche's criticisms, as reason has *a place* in moral thinking (*MC*, 1–2). He then limits his discussion to figures in this tradition, with no further mention of Nietzsche. In *Innocence and Experience* Hampshire again contrasts the philosophical tradition with Nietzsche, whose "error" is having seen no need for morality or politics, and having nothing useful to say about "averting the destruction of humanity" (*IE*, 156–57). Instead, Hampshire drifts toward Taylor's conclusion: that a Nietzschean ethic of life ultimately is destructive of life. Rather than go the route of Taylor, toward a barely articulated transcendentalism and spiritualism, which Hampshire's materialism and atheism do not allow, he seeks a universal morality that is defensible in light of his other commitments.

As for the bases of Hampshire's morality, reason is assumed to be insufficient for establishing an uncontroversial morality (*MC*, 1).[35] Though it is insufficient, reason is nevertheless important for one *layer* of morality—the thin, universal, public, articulate, accessible layer. It is less important for the second layer of morality—the much thicker, parochial, individual, imaginative, less articulate, and less accessible layer. (Nietzsche and relativists are distinguished by their denial of the first layer of morality.) The two layers are balanced imperfectly, and reason is insufficient for determining the balance. Further, the needs, desires, and capacities that we experience, even those that appear to be shared by all humans and to be most basic, *under*determine a comprehensive morality. They leave nearly every question unanswered, dictating few if any values, ideals, conventions, lifestyles, or social arrangements (*MC,* 155). Nevertheless, although admittedly problematical, morality is said to involve a "stripping down procedure," in which we attempt to identify that which is most basic and necessary for human life, if not at all times then at least at present, beneath the surface contingencies of local custom and individual idiosyncrasy (*MC,* 129).[36] But even here, Hampshire acknowledges, we encounter difficulties, as we must make assumptions regarding what constitutes a good life, and which among our conflicting desires and aspirations to view as essential or to ascribe priority. And we must decide whether to accept what is regarded as basic and necessary for humans or seek to alter these.

Hampshire wavers in his discussions of human needs, variously emphasizing their universality and their diversity. Beneath these equivocations is his distinction between the two layers of morality—that concerning the naked human, the "raw and basic necessities which are common to the whole species," and that concerning the clothed human, necessities arising within distinct ways of life (*MC,* 142). The most basic necessities (e.g., food, clean water and air, usually shelter and clothing) and experiences (e.g., birth, childhood, adolescence, old age, and death) give a general outline to human life. But the outline is so general as to allow countless values and ways of life (*MC,* 143). A small number of moral injunctions and prohibitions may be defended with reference to such human constants, but most cannot be, as they do not follow necessarily from them but only from a particular, contingent way of life.

It is regarding the narrow domain of basic, universal needs, of common interests and aspirations, identified as part of our nature, that we expect convergence in moral beliefs, rejecting beliefs that are counter to these needs as mistaken or indefensible. On all other matters—the thicker layer of culture, convention, and way of life—we expect divergence and have difficulty ruling out, by any definitive or uncontroversial means, disagreement and distinctiveness. Evoking Hobbes and especially Spinoza, Hampshire assumes the preservation of human life to be the priority of every reasonable individual and, hence, ascribes it highest value (*MC*, 96, 154). This is said to provide independent grounds for evaluating moralities, as those that lead to the destruction of life or to great misery and degradation can be regarded, by definition, as immoral. The fundamental, universal layer of morality, then, is concerned only with fair procedures, minimal standards of decency and civility, and control of "destructive impulses" (*MC*, 168). Recourse to such impulses would be a relapse into the state of nature, since morality is a *response* to nature and its function is to relieve us of this state. Since this layer of morality is meant to sustain human life, it is only felt as burdensome or limiting by those individuals at odds with human life.

The second, thicker layer, that of more specific values and ways of life, even if viewed as admirable and chosen by us, often will seem burdensome and limiting, as contrary desires cannot be satisfied and potentials cannot be realized. Recourse to a "balanced life" does not make morality less burdensome and limiting, as this ideal is only one of many. It discourages the exclusions entailed by commitment and specialization, and the sacrifices accompanying intense pursuit of goals and possibilities, encouraging instead that individuals limit themselves to moderate, familiar, low-risk lives (*MC*, 151).

When it comes to specifying the content of universal morality, Hampshire is brief, even though he presents it as modest and uncontroversial. As noted, he mainly emphasizes proceduralism and civility, as indispensable for solving conflicts without violence, and also attention to vital needs. Presumably morality would include minimal social protections, such as the relief of hunger and treatment of illness, and legal protections and rights, such as safety from assault. But, as Hampshire himself is keenly aware, even such "minimal" protections and institutions raise a host of conflicting interpretations, such as what constitutes fairness, need, wellness, and safety. Interpreting these notions leads one to the thicker layer of morality, introducing more specific and substantive, and therefore more controversial, assumptions and commitments.

Moreover, even seemingly basic needs and common aspirations, Hampshire concedes, can be posited only if we limit our attention to "normal human beings" living in "normal society" (*MC*, 7, 143). Such a concession acknowledges that some of the most "basic" needs are not basic for all, and positing them as basic entails that we view those not sharing them as abnormal or less human. To do so is to join thinkers such as Martha Nussbaum, as discussed in the previous chapter. On the other hand, perhaps this forces us only to view the incorrigible brute or self-destructive individual as abnormal, something we seldom hesitate to do.[37]

Yet Hampshire goes so far as to say that a community that attached no exceptional value to human life or did not recoil from killing would—as it should—be seen as "sub-human" (MC, 95). As intuitively sensible as this may seem to moderns, it overlooks such glaring exceptions as pre-Christian Roman civilization. Indeed, Arendt herself seeks to resurrect a premodern politics in which glory, rather than life, is the highest value. And Taylor claims that an ethic of life, if it denies that which transcends life, risks turning against life, and has insufficient resources with which to condemn impulses destructive of life. Moreover, Taylor believes that an ethic of life lacks sufficient resources for a *meaningful* life.

Hampshire's ethic of life is impoverished when he sees life and nature as less rich and layered than he sometimes finds them to be. Hampshire assumes there to be nothing higher than life, but he does not match Nietzsche in plumbing the depth and density of life. This dovetails with his tendency to sharply contrast passion and reason, and conflict and consensus, with passion undermining reason and conflict undermining consensus. In doing so, passion is equated with unthinking conflict, and the body is portrayed more crudely than it is elsewhere in his thought. This encourages Hampshire to see politics as wholly procedural, with the cold machinery of government containing clashes, muting hostilities, and regulating passions.

Instead, Hampshire's politics could give more attention to the subtle modification of passions, which he begins to do with his notion of "reflective passions" (MC, 162). Modification of passions, in order to facilitate engagement and compromise, does appear in his emphasis on *civility,* more than reason, in politics and discussion. It appears most suggestively in his characterization of liberals as having a "passion for civility within conflict."[38] Suggestions such as these provide resources for cultivating ethical sensibilities that complement Hampshire's emphasis on basic needs and fair procedures in morality and politics, an orientation that by itself is insufficient but remains a promising beginning.

In sum, unlike many contemporary thinkers, including those who emphasize the body, Hampshire neither avoids reference to universal needs nor elaborates a substantive conception of need. This places him between Foucault and Nussbaum, as I understand them. Rather, he cautiously identifies universal needs and seeks a morality stemming from them. But at the same time, he insists that a morality rooted in such needs will be radically insufficient for organizing communities and guiding individual lives, and that it will not eliminate social conflict or lead to an inclusive social order. Indeed, attempting to arrive at a universal morality of any substance would stifle individual development and cultural transformation (*MC*, 28–29). Nevertheless, we can refer to aspects of human nature that are the *least problematical*, we can identify the needs and aspirations that appear to be *most constant* and on which we are *most likely* to converge (*MC*, 127). Such an orientation can be contrasted with those not haunted by Sade, and thus far less cautious in their identification of needs and aspirations and positing of goods.[39]

Hampshire's moral universalism is challenging precisely because it remains in tension with his pluralism. He does not seek a metaphysical or metatheoretical position from which to alleviate this tension, or from which to secure a final, uncontroversial settlement. Rather, he emphasizes the extent to which each of us *experiences* varying and unvarying needs, and conflicting senses of what is conventional and natural, and thus the pull of both pluralism and universalism. He urges us to allow their coexistence as we attempt to balance them. Any balance is understood to be tentative and encourages consideration of alternative balances. Such qualifications, equivocations, and hesitations are not weaknesses of Hampshire's position but rather are its strengths.

Hampshire leaves us, then, with the paradoxical lesson that it is human nature both to experience conflict and to attempt to overcome it. Attempts to overcome it are in conflict with other aspects of human nature, and with certain individual natures. Accepting this paradox is difficult, and for many it is no doubt disappointing, but genuine self-consciousness requires that it be accepted. It is because Hampshire has so lucidly explored this paradox that his work pays revisit.

NOTES

1. Reviews of Hampshire's writings by moral and political philosophers are usually strong in their praise, yet Hampshire is seldom engaged in current discussions and is often not even acknowledged. See Ronald Dworkin, "The High Cost of Virtue," *New York Review of Books,* 24 October 1985, 37–39; William K. Frankena, review of *Morality and Conflict,* by Stuart Hampshire, *Ethics* 95 (April 1985): 740–43; David Luban, review of *Innocence and Experience,* by Stuart Hampshire, *Journal of Philosophy* 88, no. 5 (May 1991): 317–25; Adam Morton, "Doing without Good Leaders," *Times Literary Supplement,* 16–22 February 1990, 164; Thomas Nagel, "Why It's So Hard to Be Good," *New York Times Book Review,* 8 April 1984, 24; Jerome Neu, review of *Innocence and Experience,* by Stuart Hampshire, *Ethics* 102 (October 1991): 155–58; Alan Ryan, "Voice of Experience," *New York Review of Books,* 1 March 1990, 34–37; T. M. Scanlon, "Local Justice," *London Review of Books,* 5 September 1985, 17–18; Michael Slote, "Observing the Conventions," *Times Literary Supplement,* 27 January 1984, 83; and Michael Walzer, "The Minimalist," *New Republic,* 22 January 1990, 39–41.

2. Stuart N. Hampshire, introduction to *Modern Writers and Other Essays* (New York: Alfred A. Knopf, 1970), xvii.

3. Quoted in Nicholas Wade, "Ethics Panel Is Guarded about Hybrid of Cow Cells," *New York Times,* 21 November 1998, sec. A, 7. For discussions similar to mine, see Jane Bennett and William Chaloupka, eds., introduction to *In the Nature of Things: Language, Politics, and the Environment* (Minneapolis: University of Minnesota Press, 1993), vii–xvi; and Jane Bennett, "Primate Visions and Alter-Tales," in *In the Nature of Things,* 250–65.

4. For an astute analysis of such developments that revises the distinction between nature and culture instead of dispensing with it, see Evelyn Fox Keller, "Nature, Nurture, and the Human Genome Project," in *The Code of Codes: Scientific and Social Issues in the Human Genome Project,* ed. Daniel J. Kevles and Leroy Hood (Cambridge: Harvard University Press, 1992), 281–99. Keller worries that the distinction is being eclipsed by that between normality and abnormality (both viewed as natural or biological, with abnormality now more susceptible to correction). Her worries are pertinent to issues I discuss later in this chapter.

5. Stuart Hampshire, *Morality and Conflict* (Cambridge: Harvard University Press, 1983), 99, 103. Hereafter cited *MC.* See my discussion of Nietzsche's conception of instinct in the previous chapter.

6. Richard Rorty, for example, discourages reference to "nature" or "human

nature." See "Texts and Lumps," in *Objectivity, Relativism, and Truth,* vol. 1 of *Philosophical Papers* (Cambridge: Cambridge University Press, 1991), 78–92.

7. Stuart Hampshire, "Disposition and Memory," in *Philosophical Essays on Freud,* ed. Richard Wollheim (Cambridge: Cambridge University Press, 1982), 77–78, 82. See my discussion in chap. 1 of Arendt's portrait of early education; for an extended analysis of this process in Europe, see Norbert Elias, *The Civilizing Process* (Oxford: Blackwell, 1994).

8 This assumption is crucial for Martha Nussbaum. See, e.g., "Non-Relative Virtues: An Aristotelian Approach," in *The Quality of Life,* ed. Martha Nussbaum and Amartya Sen (Oxford: Clarendon Press, 1993), 242–69.

9. As mentioned in the introduction, in addition to Rorty, Judith Butler displays this tendency, with her gift for deconstruction leading her to be reluctant to refer to anything independent of language and convention, a tendency modified slightly in her recent writings. Compare *Gender Trouble: Feminism and the Subversion of Identity* (New York: Routledge, 1990) to *The Psychic Life of Power: Theories in Subjection* (Stanford: Stanford University Press, 1997). An excellent criticism of this tendency is found in Timothy V. Kaufman-Osborn, "Fashionable Subjects: On Judith Butler and the Causal Idioms of Postmodern Feminist Theory," *Political Research Quarterly* 50, no. 3 (September 1997): 649–74.

10. Leslie Paul Thiele characterizes negative, positive, and postmodern freedom as concerned with willful control of nature, whereas I emphasize the limits to control and am concerned more with experimental intervention (Hampshire's emphases waver). See Leslie Paul Thiele, "Heidegger on Freedom: Political Not Metaphysical," *American Political Science Review* 88, no. 2 (June 1994): 278–91.

11. Hampshire's distinction between nature and convention is analogous to Arendt's distinction between the private and the public. In both distinctions freedom and action are located in the second terms (convention and the public), but the distinctions themselves are contingent as they are destabilized by freedom and action. A weakness in Arendt's distinction between necessity and freedom (which is also close to Hampshire's distinction between nature and convention) is her failure to acknowledge its contingency.

12. Stuart Hampshire, *Freedom of the Individual,* expanded ed. (Princeton: Princeton University Press, 1975), 80–81. Hereafter cited *FI.*

13. An importantly similar portrait of situated, limited, embodied thinking and acting (an "analytic of finitude") is found in Michel Foucault, *The Order of Things: An Archeology of the Human Sciences* (New York: Vintage Books, 1994), 312–18.

14 Stuart Hampshire, "Sade," in *Modern Writers and Other Essays,* 56–57. Hereafter cited S.

15. Peter Weiss, *The Persecution and Assassination of Jean-Paul Marat as Performed by the Inmates of the Asylum of Charenton under the Direction of the Marquis de Sade,* trans. Geoffrey Skelton (New York: Atheneum, 1981).

16. Stuart Hampshire, "The Theatre of Sade," in *Modern Writers and Other Essays*, 64

17. In *Forbidden Knowledge: From Prometheus to Pornography* (San Diego: Harcourt Brace, 1996), 227–99, Roger Shattuck insists that responsible thinkers should have no truck with Sade, as he "belongs among the greatest immoralists capable of stimulating homicidal madness in warped minds" and, no less, encourages "perversions centered on anal intercourse" (268, 287). Shattuck lists Barthes, Bataille, Beauvoir, Foucault, Horkheimer and Adorno, Klossowski, Kundera, and Pasolini as uncritical celebrants of Sade. Rather than challenge his readings, I wish only to note that Hampshire exemplifies critical engagement, demonstrating how Sade *contributes* to ethical thinking.

18. Stuart Hampshire, "A Kind of Materialism," in *Freedom of Mind* (Princeton: Princeton University Press, 1971), 210–31. Hereafter cited KM. Hampshire is not explicit in his ontology but conveys a mechanistic conception of being. Comparison of his materialism with Nietzsche's would center on the former's emphasis on stasis and the latter's emphasis on fluidity. (Nietzsche declares that nature is always "unfinished," alluding to Genesis 2:3, in which the Lord declares on the seventh day that the heavens and earth are finished.) Stated crudely, Hampshire's is more Newtonian while Nietzsche's is more Darwinian. Both thinkers presume (as do Arendt and Taylor) that being exceeds mastery and comprehension. Yet at many points Hampshire's suggestions of mechanism and stasis lead him to regard nature as unchanging material to be effectively mastered. This then seeps into his discussions of body techniques, suggesting that our bodies can be tinkered with mechanically in order to bring them in line with our thinking.

19. Descartes is identified as the paradigmatic extra-materialist and Hobbes as the paradigmatic crass materialist. The latter identification overlooks Hobbes's insights regarding nature and artifice and the constitutive and transformative effects of thinking. These are discussed carefully in Samantha Frost, "Reading the Body: Hobbes, Body Politics, and the Task of Political Theory," in *Vocations of Political Theory*, ed. John Tambornino and Jason A. Frank (Minneapolis: University of Minnesota Press, 2000).

20. Rorty approaches Hampshire's materialism—explaining that we need not posit two categories of phenomena in order to have two (or many more) categories of explanation, such as the physical and the psychological—in Richard Rorty, "Non-reductive Physicalism," in *Objectivity, Relativism, and Truth*, 113–25.

21. Take, e.g., the increasing evidence that serial violent offenders often suffered brain injury early in life and that medication profoundly reduces their level of aggression. See Malcolm Caldwell, "Damaged," *New Yorker*, 24 February–3 March 1997, 132–47.

22. As discussed in the previous chapter, Nietzsche was, once again, before his time, when recounting in *Ecce Homo* the extent to which he incorporated such materialism into reflection on his earlier thinking and into his daily living.

23. See Margalit Fox, "With Prozac, the Rose Garden Has Hidden Thorns," *New York Times*, 4 October 1998, 3.

24. "To show the connection between knowledge of various degrees and freedom of various degrees is the principal purpose of [*Thought and Action*]," which laid the groundwork for Hampshire's subsequent writings. Stuart Hampshire, *Thought and Action*, 2d ed. (Notre Dame: University of Notre Dame Press, 1982), 133. Hereafter cited *TA*.

25. The emphasis on explanation need not be reduced to behaviorism or prediction, given the constitutive role of thinking in subjectivity and action. Moreover, explaining processes of thought may not allow us to explain thinking *as it proceeds*, due to its delicate, often unprecedented quality.

26. The portrait is closer to that of Gerald C. MacCallum Jr., "Negative and Positive Liberty," *Philosophical Review* 76 (1967): 312–34; and closer still to Michel Foucault, "The Ethics of the Concern of the Self as a Practice of Freedom," in *Ethics, Subjectivity, and Truth*, ed. Paul Rabinow, trans. Robert Hurley (New York: New Press, 1997), 281–301.

27. Michel Foucault, "What Is Enlightenment? " in *Ethics, Subjectivity, and Truth*, 315–16.

28. Stuart Hampshire, "Sincerity and Single-Mindedness," in *Freedom of Mind*, 232. Hereafter cited SSM.

29. Foucault conveys the disciplinary character of such imperatives for self-monitoring in "About the Beginning of the Hermeneutics of the Self," *Political Theory* 21, no. 2 (May 1993): 198–227.

30. A preliminary discussion of techniques and "technical education" is found in Marcel Mauss, "Techniques of the Body," *Economy and Society* 2, no. 1 (February 1973): 70–88. For a useful discussion of this essay, see Ian Hunter, "Mind Games and Body Techniques," *Southern Review* 26, no. 2 (July 1993): 172–85.

31. In isolated matters of less import or consequence, compartmentalization is often the best strategy. Does any of us not secretly despise a particular colleague or neighbor with whom we are cordial on a daily basis? As long as we submerge these feelings, we should be fine.

32. See "Rehabilitating Sex Offenders," National Public Radio's *All Things Considered*, 30 July 1998. Hampshire acknowledges such *Brave New World* or *Clockwork Orange* possibilities, in which techniques are increasingly employed for governing subjects (*FI*, 91–92; *MC*, 83–84). My objection to this program stems from my commitment not to materialism but to liberalism. As a materialist, I acknowledge that such techniques may be appropriate for modifying desires. A more liberal approach would give subjects a greater part in specifying the goals to be achieved and in selecting and practicing the techniques. And it would not vilify subjects, especially when the crimes are so ambiguous.

33. See Carl Schmitt, *The Concept of the Political,* trans. George Schwab, ed. Tracy Strong (Chicago: University of Chicago Press, 1996).

34. Stuart Hampshire, *Innocence and Experience* (Cambridge: Harvard University Press, 1989), 109. Hereafter cited *IE*.

35. Hampshire describes Rawls's implicit Platonism, which assumes that reason can yield harmony and stability by subduing conflicting desires, as perpetuating nothing less than "an ancient and disastrous illusion." Stuart Hampshire, "Liberalism: The New Twist," *New York Review of Books,* 12 August 1993, 45.

36. Relatedly, Hampshire distinguishes "thought-dependent" desires, which are bound up with concepts and which emerge from reflection, from preconceptual, prereflective desires, such as hunger and thirst (*FI,* 37, 47). Desires are not only modified by thought, Hampshire maintains, but also often are *diversified* by it, making our "natural dispositions . . . indefinitely variable in accordance with variable conceptions of these dispositions" (*MC,* 145–46). This is in contrast to Nietzsche's emphasis on the extent to which concepts and reflection serve to *unify* desires, making them more consonant with those of others.

37. In *Innocence and Experience* Hampshire focuses his opposition on "unmitigated evil and nastiness" such as Nazism (something *he experienced,* as his military duties during World War II included interrogating German officers held captive [8]).

38. Hampshire, "Liberalism: The New Twist," 47.

39. Stephen Macedo's "judgmental liberalism," e.g., maintains that "decent, elevated forms of human sexuality require a self-restraint and moderation that are undermined by simplistic celebrations of liberation from inherited constraints, celebrations that ignore the potentially tyrannical nature of sexual passion." Consequently, "self-control" is properly encouraged by social pressure and "public policies that gently and unobtrusively promote better over worse ways of life, and that elevate and stabilize our sexual lives." Stephen Macedo, "Sexuality and Liberty: Making Room for Nature and Tradition?" in *Sex, Preference, and Family: Essays on Law and Nature,* ed. David M. Estlund and Martha C. Nussbaum (New York: Oxford University Press, 1997), 86, 93, 97. For a discussion of the regulation of sexuality that shares many of my concerns see Michael Warner, *The Trouble with Normal* (New York: Free Press, 1999).

CONCLUSION

THE RETURN OF CORPOREALITY

What we used to call the "body" and "flesh" is so much more rich!
—Friedrich Nietzsche

The corporeal turn is also a *return of* corporeality, of aspects of embodiment that have been submerged in much of contemporary political theory. But it is not simply a return to previous understandings, as it must build on recent intellectual developments and acknowledge the extent to which corporeality has been, and continues to be, transformed. The corporeal turn goes beyond the linguistic turn, retaining many of its insights while modifying its suppositions and altering its emphases. Just as the heightened appreciation of language was politicized, illuminating previously neglected dimensions of politics and political thinking, so must appreciation of corporeality be politicized. Although the linguistic turn has tended to occlude crucial aspects of embodiment, appreciation of language and of corporeality can enhance and deepen that of the other.

This involves attending to *layers* of thought and action commonly passed over, and understanding thinking and politics to occur on multiple, related, nonidentical levels. Doing so stresses the inherent depth, openness, and instability of thinking and politics.[1] This is in contrast, as I have emphasized, to portraits of thinking and politics that presume, or pursue, purity, transparency, and harmony. Attention to corporeality challenges these ideals, and upholding them limits attention to corporeality.

As we have seen, many political concepts are defined in relation to the body, which then becomes a source of their instability. Despite such instability, certain categories and divisions—most fundamentally, that of "mind" and "body"—persist. They are unsettled and redefined, and take on new inflections and valences, without disappearing. Moreover, attention to "the body" soon widens to include many things. In order to convey the range of issues involved, my discussions have themselves alternated between references to embodiment and corporeality; to affect, passion, and emotion; to naturalism and materialism; and to discipline and techniques. Yet the simpler approach—confining oneself to a single dimension of corporeality, without tracing its relations to other dimensions—is insufficient. My broader approach may lead into a morass, but it is, ultimately, an *unavoidable* morass, one that is even more problematically avoided by searching for dry ground removed from it.

Furthermore, although isolating the body as a topic of concern may seem to reinforce a mind-body dualism, it is more the case that failing to attend to the body does so. It does so by suggesting that something wholly apart from the body, something extramaterial or not-body, can be isolated and given primacy. Those thinkers—to an extent Arendt, and more clearly Habermas and Rawls—whose ideal of political thinking implies disembodiment risk doing this. In comparison, my course seems more promising.

Examining the presence of corporeality in the thinking of Arendt, Taylor, Nietzsche, and Hampshire is both an end in itself and a means to a larger end—of identifying issues, raising questions, glimpsing possibilities, and making interventions. This book itself attempts to modify materialism by interpreting important thinkers with attention to aspects of their thinking that receive comparatively little attention. Exploring the significance for their thinking of corporeality reveals the extent to which it extends to the farthest reaches of politics.

Discussing these thinkers in combination also weakens familiar groupings. For example, Arendt is often appreciated as an exemplary political thinker, deeply committed to freedom and plurality. But in important respects, her limited attention to issues of the body, and her ideal of a purified politics, carry apolitical tendencies at odds with freedom and plurality.

By depoliticizing vast domains of life, Arendt makes politics an extremely rare, nearly impossible activity. In contrast, Nietzsche is often seen as largely apolitical. Yet by probing the crucial role of affect and discipline in thinking and culture, he becomes a deeply political thinker, one who explores dimensions of politics ignored by many.

Reading Taylor alongside Hampshire is also instructive, as it further unsettles the "liberal-communitarian debate." A standard claim in this debate is that liberals mistakenly presume a disembodied, atomized self, either rationalist or voluntarist, rather than an embodied, situated, passionate self, constituted in large part by attachments and encumbrances.[2] But with Hampshire we find a liberal whose thought *begins* with a conception of an embodied, situated, passionate self, one with multiple, complex attachments and encumbrances. Elaboration of the complex constitution of such a self underlies this liberal's construals of freedom and individuality.

Taylor, regarded as a leading communitarian, is found to have a conception of the self that at points resembles Hampshire's. Where it does not, it presumes a teleology intrinsic to the embodied self, involving a number of contestable assumptions. Communitarians, especially if Taylor is their model, must stress embodiment when emphasizing encumbered selves as they do, but must ignore embodiment when emphasizing stability and harmony as they do. Such selective appreciation of embodiment is unavoidable. Thus the difference between liberal and communitarian orientations rests, significantly, on their different presumptions regarding the body.[3]

Finally, examining two thinkers associated with the primacy of language in human affairs—Nietzsche, who is often credited for his postmetaphysical, linguistic turn, and Taylor, who is regarded as a leading interpretivist—problematizes these associations. It does so since, as we have seen, both are deeply attentive to corporeality, and this shapes their conceptions of language and interpretation. Indeed, their orientations to the body influence the ways in which they *use* language, their writing styles and strategies. Appreciating the relation of language to corporeality underscores the *somatic effects* of writing, as a technique tapping into levels of thinking and being below the register of language. In conceiving of writing as a technique of the body, the linguistic and corporeal turns converge.

Recall my discussion of Nietzsche's writing style, with its intense, fluctuating forms of provocation, excitation, accusation, seduction, and experimentation. In this case, writing is a means to incite certain experiences and sensations, especially those of discomfort, discord, and dissonance. Or consider Taylor's coaxing, gentle style, which patiently works to articulate implicit understandings and inchoate sentiments. Taylor draws the reader along, reflecting his attempt to foster the attunement he thinks already awaits us as possibility. Consider further the controlled, cool manner that Hampshire reserves for the most arousing and disturbing matters, one that reflects his wariness toward the potential dangers of unsubdued passions. My style has been, perhaps, a combination of these, resembling Taylor's at points, without his assumption of eventual attunement, and Hampshire's at others, sharing his wariness toward certain levels of excitation. And I have oscillated between Hampshire's efforts to neatly formulate matters and Nietzsche's insistence of the insufficiency of such formulations.

I end with two additional points: the value of pleasure and the politics of materialism. At points I may appear to uphold pleasure as the highest value, and to be especially concerned with sexual pleasure. I do follow Nietzsche in writing against tendencies of thought—variously found in such thinkers as Plato, Aristotle, Paul, Augustine, and Kant—that are wary of pleasure and desire, tendencies that continue to exert cultural influence today. But self-conscious materialism does not necessarily give priority to pleasure, and certainly not to sexual pleasure, as it involves critical attention to the formation, character, and priority of pleasures and desires. In some circumstances—such as our present context of relentless, manic consumerism—self-conscious materialism may lead one to modify these influences through disciplines and restraints. The resources for responding critically to such influences need not be, *pace* Taylor, transcendental, extramaterial, or spiritual. Rather, *within* self-conscious materialism there are resources—insights, terms, suppositions, images, tactics, techniques—for challenging them.

It must also be mentioned that the commitment implicit in my discussions, drawn in part from Nietzsche and Hampshire, to struggle to identify occluded or unrealized possibilities of being may be less pertinent today.

In large, complex, rapidly changing societies such as ours, in which there often seem to be an endless, overwhelming number of possibilities, the challenge often seems to be less that of unsettling one's orientation than of subduing the sensation of constant disorientation. In such a situation, one might adopt disciplines and tactics that limit oneself, in order to focus on select activities and experiences. Alternatively, one might probe more deeply for the hidden values and stable selves sustaining contemporary forms of diversity, mobility, and social change.

Another book could be written on the political and policy implications of a corporeal turn, especially regarding techniques of the body. Making a corporeal turn—and adopting self-conscious materialism—does not itself entail any particular politics. It draws attention to certain concerns and dimensions of politics, and shapes treatment of them, while leaving open many political questions. I have contended that ideals of community begin to give way once the body is taken seriously, and that attention to shared needs and varying desires lends itself to liberal pluralism, but the relationships are not ones of strict entailment. My liberal pluralist leanings underlie my reservations regarding corporeal politics at odds with freedom and plurality, such as the rehabilitation of sexual offenders discussed in the previous chapter, and the increasing reliance on knowledge of the body to govern subjects, to intervene more effectively to normalize individuals and manage populations. Turning to corporeality thus draws attention to subterranean strategies by which freedom and plurality are diminished.

I have also claimed that many of us are already self-conscious materialists in our daily lives, but that our materialism becomes less self-conscious as we theorize and practice politics. There are, however, political theorists and actors who strongly resist the implications of materialism and instead seek to reinstate extramaterialism. Consider the return to "faith-based healing," in opposition to secular trends in medicine and psychiatry, to reform drug addicts and juvenile delinquents. Organizations practicing this maintain that religious faith alone can heal addiction, rejecting the "therapeutic notion that it's a disease." They use intensive disciplines and tactics of the self (involving arduous labor and corporal punishment, often resulting in serious injury) to reform subjects by modifying subjectivity—ultimately "transforming lives." Refusing to understand these conditions by reference to factors such as genetic predisposition or the physiology of addiction, practitioners invoke extramaterialist notions such as "weakness of will," "soul," and "salvation." Programs are designed to induce subjects to understand themselves, and to experience their cravings, through these notions.[4]

Techniques such as these can, of course, be given an alternative, materialist reading. Self-conscious materialists, then, not only elaborate a position tacitly held by many but also challenge large numbers of extramaterialists. Far from being "merely academic," the politics of materialism could hardly be of greater practical import.

Having begun to spell out the corporeal turn and the return of corporeality should be enough for now. This should allow their significance—for thinking and for corporeality—to begin to take effect.

NOTES

1. Appreciation of the depth of thinking and politics, especially of that which exceeds consciousness, *may* proceed in idioms other than that of psychoanalysis. Although I have mentioned it only in passing, psychoanalysis has been of great value in its emphasis on the unconscious, but it should not monopolize this domain. (Many of those who have gained distance from psychoanalysis have moved toward an emphasis on language, in the manner that I have argued is problematical.)

2. Michael Sandel, who has been most influential in framing this debate, now acknowledges its limitations. Although his communitarianism has evolved into republicanism, a dichotomy between "encumbered" and "voluntarist" selves remains central to his thought. See Michael J. Sandel, *Democracy's Discontent: America in Search of a Public Philosophy* (Cambridge: Harvard University Press, 1996).

3. Attention to the body serves to reconfigure a number of other debates. E.g., as discussed in the previous chapter, consideration of the universality and the diversity of particular needs modifies the common opposition between ethical universalists and cultural pluralists. And scientific advances, especially in genetics, are likely to have profound implications for conceptions of equality, freedom, individuality, and self-making.

4. Texas initially led this development, with then Governor George W. Bush's 1997 Faith in Action initiative. Since then, fifty-eight churches have registered as drug treatment programs—monitored only by a Christian oversight agency—with plans to publicly fund the programs in coming years. Since this conclusion was drafted, the macrop-

olitical significance of such micropolitical experiments has grown, as President Bush's Office of Faith-Based Action is devising ways to seed the Texas model nationwide. See Hanna Rosin, "Putting Faith in a Social Service Role," *Washington Post*, 5 May 2000, A1.

BIBLIOGRAPHY

Ackerman, Robert. *Nietzsche: A Frenzied Look*. Amherst: University of Massachusetts Press, 1990.

Ahern, Daniel R. *Nietzsche as Cultural Physician*. University Park: Pennsylvania University Press, 1995.

Almond, Gabriel, and Sidney Verba. *The Civic Culture*. Boston: Little, Brown, 1965.

Ansell-Pearson, Keith. *Nietzsche contra Rousseau*. Cambridge: Cambridge University Press, 1991.

Arendt, Hannah. "What Is Existenz Philosophy?" *Partisan Review* 13, no. 1 (Winter 1946): 34–56.

_____. "Understanding and Politics." *Partisan Review* 20, no. 4 (1953): 391–92.

_____. *Between Past and Future*. New York: Penguin Books, 1954.

_____. *The Human Condition*. Chicago: University of Chicago Press, 1958.

_____. *On Revolution*. New York: Penguin Books, 1963.

_____. *The Life of the Mind: Thinking*. New York: Harcourt Brace, 1978.

_____. *The Life of the Mind: Willing*. New York: Harcourt Brace, 1978.

_____. *Lectures on Kant's Political Philosophy*. Edited by Ronald Beiner. Chicago: University of Chicago Press, 1982.

_____. "Thinking and Moral Considerations." *Social Research* 51, no. 1–2 (1984): 7–37.

Armstrong, T., ed. *American Bodies: Cultural Histories of the Physique*. New York: New York University Press, 1996.

Asad, Talal. *Genealogies of Religion: Discipline and Reasons of Power in Christianity and Islam*. Baltimore: Johns Hopkins University Press, 1993.

Barker, Francis. *The Tremulous Private Body: Essays on Subjection*. Ann Arbor: University of Michigan Press, 1995.

Benhabib, Seyla. *The Reluctant Modernism of Hannah Arendt*. Thousand Oaks, Calif.: Sage, 1996.

Bennett, Jane. "Primate Visions and Alter-Tales." In *In the Nature of Things: Language, Politics, and the Environment,* edited by Jane Bennett and William Chaloupka, 250–65. Minneapolis: University of Minnesota Press, 1993.

Bennett, Jane, and William Chaloupka, ed. *In the Nature of Things: Language, Politics, and the Environment.* Minneapolis: University of Minnesota Press, 1993.

Berlin, Isaiah. *Four Essays on Liberty.* Oxford: Oxford University Press, 1969.

————. Introduction to *Philosophy in an Age of Pluralism: The Philosophy of Charles Taylor in Question,* edited by James Tully, 1–3. Cambridge: Cambridge University Press, 1994.

Bermudez, Jose Luis, Anthony Marcel, and Naomi Eilan, eds. *The Body and the Self.* Cambridge: MIT Press, 1995.

Bernstein, Richard J. "Rethinking the Social and the Political." In *Philosophical Profiles: Essays in a Pragmatic Mode.* Philadelphia: University of Pennsylvania Press, 1986.

Bersani, Leo. *Homos.* Cambridge: Harvard University Press, 1995.

Blakeslee, Sandra. "Complex and Hidden Brain in the Gut Makes Cramps, Butterflies, and Valium." *New York Times,* 22 March 1996, sec. C, 1, 3.

Blondel, Eric. *Nietzsche—The Body and Culture: Philosophy as a Philological Genealogy.* Translated by Sean Hand. Stanford: Stanford University Press, 1991.

Brewer, Bill. "Bodily Awareness and the Self." In *The Body and the Self,* edited by Jose Luis Bermudez, Anthony Marcel, and Naomi Eilan, 291–309. Cambridge: MIT Press, 1995.

Brown, Peter. *The Body and Society: Men, Women, and Sexual Renunciation in Early Christianity.* New York: Columbia University Press, 1988.

Butler, Judith. *Gender Trouble: Feminism and the Subversion of Identity.* New York: Routledge, 1990.

————. *Bodies That Matter: On the Discursive Limits of "Sex."* New York: Routledge, 1993.

————. *The Psychic Life of Power: Theories in Subjection.* Stanford: Stanford University Press, 1997.

Butler, Judith, and William Connolly. "Politics, Power, and Ethics: A Discussion." *Theory and Event* 4, no. 2 (2000). http://muse.jhu.edu/journals/theory_&_event/v004/4.2butler.html

Bynum, Caroline. "Why All the Fuss about the Body? A Medievalist's Perspective." *Critical Inquiry* 22 (Autumn 1995): 1–33.

Caldwell, Malcolm. "Damaged." *New Yorker,* 24 February–3 March 1997, 132–47.

Cameron, Loren. *Body Alchemy: Transsexual Portraits.* Pittsburgh: Cleis Press, 1996.

Campo, Rafael. *What the Body Told.* Durham, N.C.: Duke University Press, 1996.

Carpentier, Alejo. *The Chase.* Translated by Alfred MacAdam. New York: Noonday Press, 1989.

Cavell, Stanley. *The Pitch of Philosophy: Autobiographical Exercises.* Cambridge: Harvard University Press, 1994.

Chauncey, George. *Gay New York: Gender, Urban Culture, and the Making of the Gay Male World, 1890–1940*. New York: Basic Books, 1994.

Clark, Andy. "Where Brain, Body, and World Collide." *Daedalus* 127, no. 2 (Spring 1998): 257–80.

Cohen, Jean. "Democracy, Difference, and the Right to Privacy." In *Democracy and Difference: Contesting the Boundaries of the Political*, edited by Seyla Benhabib, 187–217. Princeton: Princeton University Press, 1996.

Connerton, Paul. *How Societies Remember*. Cambridge: Cambridge University Press, 1989.

Connolly, William E. "Taylor, Foucault, and Otherness." *Political Theory* 13, no. 3 (August 1985): 365–76.

———. *Politics and Ambiguity*. Madison: University of Wisconsin Press, 1987.

———. *The Ethos of Pluralization*. Minneapolis: University of Minnesota Press, 1995.

———. *Why I Am Not a Secularist*. Minneapolis: University of Minnesota Press, 1999.

Deleuze, Gilles. *Nietzsche and Philosophy*. Translated by Hugh Tomlinson. New York: Columbia University Press, 1983.

Dietz, Mary. "Hannah Arendt and Feminist Politics." In *Feminist Interpretations and Political Theory*, edited by Mary Lyndon Shanley and Carole Pateman, 232–52. Cambridge, England: Polity Press, 1991.

Disch, Lisa Jane. *Hannah Arendt and the Limits of Philosophy*. Ithaca: Cornell University Press, 1994.

Dworkin, Ronald. "The High Cost of Virtue." *New York Review of Books*, 24 October 1985, 37–39.

Dzur, Albert W. "Liberal Perfectionism and Democratic Participation." *Polity* 30, no. 4 (Summer 1998): 667–90.

Elias, Norbert. *The Civilizing Process*. Oxford: Blackwell, 1994.

Elshtain, Jean Bethke. "Introduction: Bodies and Politics." In *Politics and the Human Body: An Assault on Dignity*, edited by Jean Bethke Elshtain and J. Timothy Cloyd, ix–xvi. Nashville: Vanderbilt University Press, 1995.

Fisher, Marc, and Sue Ann Pressley. "Crisis of Sexuality Launched Strange Journey." *Washington Post*, 29 March 1997, A1.

Flathman, Richard E. *Toward a Liberalism*. Ithaca: Cornell University Press, 1989.

Foucault, Michel. *Language, Countermemory, Practice*. Edited by Donald Blouchard. Ithaca: Cornell University Press, 1977.

———. *Discipline and Punish*. Translated by Alan Sheridan. New York: Vintage Books, 1979.

———. *The Foucault Reader*. Edited by Paul Rabinow. New York: Pantheon, 1984.

———. "About the Beginning of the Hermeneutics of the Self." *Political Theory* 21, no. 2 (May 1993): 198–227.

———. *The Order of Things: An Archeology of the Human Sciences*. New York: Vintage Books, 1994.

————. *Ethics, Subjectivity, and Truth.* Edited by Paul Rabinow, translated by Robert Hurley. New York: New Press, 1997.

Fox, Margalit. "With Prozac, the Rose Garden Has Hidden Thorns." *New York Times,* 4 October 1998, 3.

Frankena, William K. Review of *Morality and Conflict,* by Stuart Hampshire. *Ethics* 95 (April 1985): 740–43.

Frost, Samantha. "Reading the Body: Hobbes, Body Politics, and the Task of Political Theory." In *Vocations of Political Theory,* edited by John Tambornino and Jason A. Frank. Minneapolis: University of Minnesota Press, 2000.

Geertz, Clifford. "The Strange Estrangement: Taylor and the Natural Sciences." In *Philosophy in an Age of Pluralism: The Philosophy of Charles Taylor in Question,* edited by James Tully, 83–95. Cambridge: Cambridge University Press, 1994.

Gendlin, Eugene T. "The Wider Role of Bodily Sense in Thought and Language." In *Giving the Body Its Due,* edited by Maxine Sheets-Johnstone, 192–207. Albany: State University of New York Press, 1992.

Giddens, Anthony. *The Transformation of Intimacy: Sexuality, Love, and Eroticism in Modern Societies.* Cambridge: Cambridge University Press, 1992.

Gide, André. *The Immoralist.* Translated by Richard Howard. New York: Vintage Books, 1996.

Goleman, Daniel. "'Wrong' Sex: A New Definition of Childhood Pain." *New York Times,* 22 March 1994, sec. B, 6–7.

Grosz, Elizabeth. *Volatile Bodies: Towards a Corporeal Feminism.* Bloomington: Indiana University Press, 1994.

Habermas, Jürgen. *The Philosophical Discourse of Modernity.* Translated by Frederick Lawrence. Cambridge: MIT Press, 1987.

————. *Postmetaphysical Thinking.* Translated by William Mark Hohengarten. Cambridge: MIT Press, 1992.

Hacking, Ian. *Representing and Intervening.* Cambridge: Cambridge University Press, 1983.

Hampshire, Stuart N. *Modern Writers and Other Essays.* New York: Alfred A. Knopf, 1970.

————. *Freedom of Mind.* Princeton: Princeton University Press, 1971.

————. *Freedom of the Individual.* Expanded ed. Princeton: Princeton University Press, 1975.

————. "Disposition and Memory." In *Philosophical Essays on Freud,* edited by Richard Wollheim, 75–91. Cambridge: Cambridge University Press, 1982.

————. *Thought and Action.* New ed. Notre Dame: University of Notre Dame Press, 1982.

————. *Morality and Conflict.* Cambridge: Harvard University Press, 1983.

————. *Innocence and Experience.* Cambridge: Harvard University Press, 1989.

———. "Liberalism: The New Twist." *New York Review of Books,* 12 August 1993, 43–47.

———. *Justice Is Conflict.* Princeton: Princeton University Press, 2000.

Hunter, Ian. "Mind Games and Body Techniques." *Southern Review* 26, no. 2 (July 1993): 172–85.

Honig, Bonnie. "Toward an Agonistic Feminism: Hannah Arendt and the Politics of Identity." In *Feminist Interpretations of Hannah Arendt,* edited by Bonnie Honig, 135–66. University Park: Pennsylvania State University Press, 1995.

Hyde, Alan. *Bodies of Law.* Princeton: Princeton University Press, 1997.

Jacobitti, Suzanne Duvall. "Thinking about the Self." In *Hannah Arendt: Twenty Years Later,* edited by Larry May and Jerome Kohn, 199–219. Cambridge: MIT Press, 1996.

Johnson, Mark. *The Body in Mind: The Bodily Basis of Meaning, Imagination, and Reason.* Chicago: University of Chicago Press, 1987.

Kafka, Franz. *The Metamorphosis, In the Penal Colony, and Other Stories.* Translated by Joachim Neurgroschel. New York: Simon & Schuster, 1993.

Kateb, George. *Hannah Arendt: Politics, Conscience, Evil.* Totowa, N.J.: Rowman & Allanhead, 1984.

Kaufman-Osborn, Timothy V. "Fashionable Subjects: On Judith Butler and the Causal Idioms of Postmodern Feminist Theory." *Political Research Quarterly* 50, no. 3 (September 1997): 649–74.

Keller, Evelyn Fox. "Nature, Nurture, and the Human Genome Project." In *The Code of Codes: Scientific and Social Issues in the Human Genome Project,* edited by Daniel J. Kevles and Leroy Hood, 281–99. Cambridge: Harvard University Press, 1992.

Kleinman, Arthur, and Byron Good, eds. *Culture and Depression: Studies in the Anthropology and Cross-Cultural Psychiatry of Affect and Disorder.* Berkeley and Los Angeles: University of California Press, 1985.

Kleinman, Arthur, and Joan Kleinman. "Somatization: The Interconnections in Chinese Society among Culture, Depressive Experiences, and the Meanings of Pain." In *Culture and Depression: Studies in the Anthropology and Cross-Cultural Psychiatry of Affect and Disorder,* edited by Arthur Kleinman and Byron Good. Berkeley and Los Angeles: University of California Press, 1985.

———. "How Bodies Remember: Social Memory and Bodily Experience of Criticism, Resistance, and Delegitimation Following China's Cultural Revolution." *New Literary History* 25 (1994): 707–23.

Kleinman, Arthur, et al. *Pain as Human Experience: An Anthropological Perspective.* Berkeley and Los Angeles: University of California Press, 1992.

Kripke, Saul A. *Wittgenstein on Rules and Private Language.* Cambridge: Harvard University Press, 1982.

Kundera, Milan. *The Book of Laughter and Forgetting.* Translated by Michael Henry Heim. New York: Penguin Books, 1980.

————. *The Unbearable Lightness of Being.* Translated by Michael Henry Heim. New York: Harper Perennial, 1984.

————. *Immortality.* Translated by Peter Kussi. New York: Harper Perennial, 1992.

————. *Identity.* Translated by Linda Asher. New York: HarperCollins, 1998.

Lacquer, Thomas. *Making Sex: Body and Gender from the Greeks to Freud.* Cambridge: Harvard University Press, 1990.

Ledoux, Joseph. *The Emotional Brain: The Mysterious Underpinnings of Emotional Life.* New York: Simon & Schuster, 1996.

Lingis, Alphonso. *Dangerous Emotions.* Berkeley and Los Angeles: University of California Press, 2000.

Luban, David. Review of *Innocence and Experience,* by Stuart Hampshire. *Journal of Philosophy* 88, no. 5 (May 1991): 317–25.

Lyotard, Jean-François. "Can Thought Go without a Body?" *Discourse* 11, no. 1 (Fall–Winter 1988–89): 74–87.

MacCallum, Gerald C., Jr. "Negative and Positive Liberty." *Philosophical Review* 76 (1967): 312–34.

MacCannell, Juliet Flower, ed. *Thinking Bodies.* Stanford: Stanford University Press, 1994.

Macedo, Stephen. "Sexuality and Liberty: Making Room for Nature and Tradition?" In *Sex, Preference, and Family: Essays on Law and Nature,* edited by David M. Estlund and Martha C. Nussbaum. New York: Oxford University Press, 1997.

Mauss, Marcel. "Techniques of the Body." *Economy and Society* 2, no. 1 (February 1973): 70–88.

McNeill, William H. *Keeping Together in Time: Dance and Drill in Human History.* Cambridge: Harvard University Press, 1995.

Morton, Adam. "Doing without Good Leaders." *Times Literary Supplement,* 16–22 February 1990, 164.

Nagel, Thomas. "Why It's So Hard to Be Good." *New York Times Book Review,* 8 April 1984, 24.

Neu, Jerome. Review of *Innocence and Experience,* by Stuart Hampshire. *Ethics* 102 (October 1991): 155–58.

Nietzsche, Friedrich. *The Will to Power.* Translated by Walter Kaufmann and R. J. Hollingdale. New York: Vintage Books, 1968.

————. *The Gay Science.* Translated by Walter Kaufmann. New York: Vintage Books, 1974 .

————. *Thus Spoke Zarathustra: A Book for None and All.* Translated by Walter Kaufmann. New York: Penguin Books, 1978.

————. *Philosophy and Truth: Selections from Nietzsche's Notebooks of the Early 1870's.* Edited and translated by Daniel Breazeale. Atlantic Highlands, N.J.: Humanities Press International, 1979.

———. *On the Genealogy of Morals.* Translated by Walter Kaufmann. New York: Vintage Books, 1989.

———. *Twilight of the Idols.* Translated by R. J. Hollingdale. New York: Penguin Books, 1990.

Nussbaum, Martha C. "Human Functioning and Social Justice: In Defense of Aristotelian Essentialism." *Political Theory* 20, no. 2 (May 1992): 202–46.

———. "Non-Relative Virtues: An Aristotelian Approach." In *The Quality of Life,* edited by Martha C. Nussbaum and Amartya Sen, 242–69. Oxford: Clarendon Press, 1993.

———. "Compassion: The Basic Social Emotion." *Social Philosophy and Policy* 13, no. 1 (Winter 1996): 27–58.

Nussbaum, Martha C., and Cass R. Sunstein. *Clones and Cloning: Facts and Fantasies.* New York: Norton, 1998.

Outram, Dorinda. *The Body and the French Revolution: Sex, Class, and Political Culture.* New Haven: Yale University Press, 1989.

Patton, Paul. "Taylor and Foucault on Power and Freedom." *Political Studies* 37 (1989): 260–76.

———. "Nietzsche and the Body of the Philosopher." In *Cartographies: Post-Structuralism and the Mapping of Bodies,* edited by R. Diprose and R. Ferrel, 43–54. Sydney: Allen & Unwin, 1991.

Pitkin, Hanna Fenichel. *The Attack of the Blob: Hannah Arendt's Concept of the Social.* Chicago: University of Chicago Press, 1998.

Putnam, Hilary. *Words and Life.* Cambridge: Harvard University Press, 1994.

"Rehabilitating Sex Offenders." National Public Radio's *All Things Considered.* 30 July 1998.

Rosin, Hanna. "Putting Faith in a Social Service Role." *Washington Post,* 5 May 2000, sec. A, 1.

Rorty, Richard. *Consequences of Pragmatism.* Minneapolis: University of Minnesota Press, 1982.

———. "Education without Dogma." *Dissent* (Spring 1989): 198–204.

———. *Contingency, Irony, and Solidarity.* Cambridge: Cambridge University Press, 1989.

———. "Feminism and Pragmatism." *Michigan Quarterly Review* (1991): 231–58.

———. *Objectivity, Relativism, and Truth.* Cambridge: Cambridge University Press, 1991.

Ryan, Alan. "Voice of Experience." *New York Review of Books,* 1 March 1990, 34–37.

Sandel, Michael J. *Democracy's Discontent: America in Search of a Public Philosophy.* Cambridge: Harvard University Press, 1996.

Scanlon, T. M. "Local Justice." *London Review of Books,* 5 September 1985, 17–18.

Scarry, Elaine. *The Body in Pain: The Making and Unmaking of the World.* New York: Oxford University Press, 1985.

Schmitt, Carl. *The Concept of the Political*. Translated by George Schwab, edited by Tracy Strong. Chicago: University of Chicago Press, 1996.

Sennett, Richard. *Flesh and Stone: The Body and the City in Western Civilization*. New York: W. W. Norton, 1994.

———. "The Social Body." *Transition* 6, no. 3 (1971): 80–98.

Schatzki, Theodore R., and Wolfgang Natter, eds. *The Social and Political Body*. New York: Guilford Press, 1996.

"The Science of Homosexuality" [symposium]. *Harvard Gay and Lesbian Review* (Winter 1997): 4, 13–30.

Shattuck, Roger. *Forbidden Knowledge: From Prometheus to Pornography*. San Diego: Harcourt Brace, 1996.

Skinner, Quentin. "Modernity and Disenchantment: Some Historical Reflections." In *Philosophy in an Age of Pluralism: The Philosophy of Charles Taylor in Question*, edited by James Tully, 37–48. Cambridge: Cambridge University Press, 1994.

Slote, Michael. "Observing the Conventions." *Times Literary Supplement*, 27 January 1984, 83.

Solomon, Robert C. "Nietzsche *ad hominem:* Perspectivism, Personality, and *Ressentiment*." In *The Cambridge Companion to Nietzsche*, edited by Bernard Magnus and Kathleen Higgins. Cambridge: Cambridge University Press, 1996,

Steinberger, Peter. "Arendt on Judgment." *American Journal of Political Science* 34, no. 3 (August 1990): 803–21.

Styron, William. *Darkness Visible: A Memoir of Madness*. New York: Vintage Books, 1990.

Tambornino, John. "Philosophy as the Mirror of Liberalism: The Politics of Richard Rorty." *Polity* 30, no. 1 (Fall 1997): 57–78.

Taylor, Charles. *Hegel and Modern Society*. Cambridge: Cambridge University Press, 1979.

———. Review of *Public and Private Morality*, edited by Stuart Hampshire. *MIND* 89, no. 356 (October 1980): 623–28.

———. "Foucault on Freedom and Truth." *Political Theory* 12, no. 2 (May 1984): 152–83.

———. "Connolly, Foucault, and Truth," *Political Theory* 13, no. 3 (August 1985): 377–85.

———. *Human Agency and Language*. Vol. 1 of *Philosophical Papers*. Cambridge: Cambridge University Press, 1985.

———. *Philosophy and the Human Sciences*. Vol. 2 of *Philosophical Papers*. Cambridge: Cambridge University Press, 1985.

———. *Sources of the Self: The Making of Modern Identity*. Cambridge: Harvard University Press, 1989.

———. "Taylor and Foucault on Power and Freedom: A Reply." *Political Studies* 37 (1989): 278–81.

————. "Embodied Agency." In *Merleau-Ponty: Critical Essays,* edited by Henry Pietersma. Washington, D.C.: University Press of America, 1989.

————. *The Ethics of Authenticity.* Cambridge: Harvard University Press, 1991.

————. *Reconciling the Solitudes: Essays on Canadian Federalism.* Montreal: McGill–Queen's University Press, 1994.

————. *Philosophical Arguments.* Cambridge: Harvard University Press, 1995.

————. "The Immanent Counter-Enlightenment." In *Canadian Political Philosophy: Contemporary Reflections,* edited by Ronald Beiner and Wayne Norman. Oxford: Oxford University Press, 2001.

Thiele, Leslie Paul. *Friedrich Nietzsche and the Politics of the Soul.* Princeton: Princeton University Press, 1990.

————. "Heidegger on Freedom: Political Not Metaphysical." *American Political Science Review* 88, no. 2 (June 1994): 278–91.

Thomson, Rosemary Garland, ed. *Freakery: Cultural Spectacles of the Extraordinary Body.* New York: New York University Press, 1996.

Thoreau, Henry David. *Walden.* New York: New American Library, 1980.

Tully, James. "Wittgenstein and Political Philosophy: Understanding Practices of Critical Reflection." *Political Theory* 17, no. 2 (May 1989): 172–204.

Turner, Bryan S. *The Body and Society: Explorations in Social Theory.* Oxford: Oxford University Press, 1984.

Villa, Dana. *Arendt and Heidegger: The Fate of the Political.* Princeton: Princeton University Press, 1996.

Wade, Nicholas. "Ethics Panel Is Guarded about Hybrid of Cow Cells." *New York Times,* 21 November 1998, sec. A, 7.

Walzer, Michael. "The Minimalist." *New Republic,* 22 January 1990, 39–41.

Warner, Michael. "The Mass Public and the Mass Subject." In *Habermas and the Public Sphere.* edited by Craig Calhoun, 377–401. Cambridge: MIT Press, 1992.

————. *Fear of a Queer Planet: Queer Politics and Social Theory.* Minneapolis: University of Minnesota Press, 1993.

————. *The Trouble with Normal.* New York: Free Press, 1999.

Warren, Mark. "Nietzsche and Weber: When Does Reason Become Power?" In *The Barbarism of Reason,* edited by A. Horowitz and T. Maley, 68–96. Toronto: University of Toronto Press, 1994.

Weiss, Peter. *The Persecution and Assassination of Jean-Paul Marat as Performed by the Inmates of the Asylum of Charenton under the Direction of the Marquis de Sade.* Translated by Geoffrey Skelton. New York: Atheneum, 1981.

White, Alan. *Within Nietzsche's Labyrinth.* New York: Routledge, 1990.

Williams, Bernard. *Ethics and the Limits of Philosophy.* Cambridge: Harvard University Press, 1985.

————. *Shame and Necessity.* Berkeley and Los Angeles: University of California Press, 1993.

————. *Making Sense of Humanity.* Cambridge: Cambridge University Press, 1995.

Wilson, James Q., and Richard J. Hernstein. *Crime and Human Nature.* New York: Simon & Schuster, 1985.

Wittgenstein, Ludwig. *Philosophical Investigations.* Translated by G. E. M. Anscombe. 3d ed. New York: Macmillan, 1958.

Wolin, Sheldon. "Hannah Arendt: Democracy and the Political." *Salmagundi* 60 (1983): 3–19.

Young, Iris Marion. "Communication and the Other: Beyond Deliberative Democracy." In *Democracy and Difference: Contesting the Boundaries of the Political,* edited by Seyla Benhabib, 120–35. Princeton: Princeton University Press, 1996.

Young-Bruehl, Elizabeth. *Mind and the Body Politic.* New York: Routledge, 1989.

Zerilli, Linda M.G. "The Arendtian Body." In *Feminist Interpretations of Hannah Arendt,* edited by Bonnie Honig, 167–93. University Park: Pennsylvania State University Press, 1995.

INDEX

ABOUT THE AUTHOR

John Tambornino received a B.A. magna cum laude in philosophy and political science from Macalester College and a Ph.D. in political science from Johns Hopkins University, where he was a James Hart Fellow and later a visiting lecturer. He is presently a fellow in the university's Center for the Study of American Government in Washington, D.C. His essays have appeared in *Polity* and the *Journal of Political Philosophy*, and he is the editor (with Jason A. Frank) of *Vocations of Political Theory*.